Principles of Islamic Spirituality

Part 1: Sufism

Principles of Islamic Spirituality

Part 1: Sufism

Shaykh Muhammad Hisham Kabbani

PUBLISHED BY THE
INSTITUTE FOR SPIRITUAL AND CULTURAL ADVANCEMENT

Published and Distributed by:

Institute for Spiritual and Cultural Advancement (ISCA)
17195 Silver Parkway, #201
Fenton, Michigan 48430 USA
Tel: (888) 278-6624
Fax: (810) 815-0518
Email: staff@naqshbandi.org
Web: http://www.naqshbandi.org

First Edition: October 2013
Principles of Islamic Spirituality, Part 1: Sufism
ISBN: 978-1-938058-21-9

PRINTED IN THE UNITED STATES OF AMERICA
15 14 13 12 11 05 06 07 08 09

Sayyidi Shaykh Muhammad Nazim Adil al-Haqqani of Cyprus (right), world leader of the Naqshbandi-Haqqani Sufi Order, with his deputy and author of this book, Shaykh Muhammad Hisham Kabbani.

Contents

About the Author i

Introduction iii

Publisher's Notes v

THE SUFIS **1**

Enlightened Community Builders 3

The Sufi Hierarchy 3

The Sufi Approach to Advancement 4

Principles of Treating the Self 5

The Doctors of Hearts 6

The Sufi Approach to Society-Building 7

Sufism and Religious Plurality 9

Emphasis on Art 10

Inner Peace, Outer Dialogue 11

SUFISM AND THE PERENNIAL CONFLICT OF GOOD AND EVIL **13**

Abstract 15

Introduction 17

Goal of the Believer: Perfection of Divine Service 18

What the Prophet Brought 20

Umm al-Ahadith: The Hadith of Jibril 21

The Second Component of *Din al-Islam*: *Iman* (Belief) 23

The Third Component of Din al-Islam: Ihsan (Perfection of Character) ... 23

The Relationship between Shari'ah and *Haqiqat* 24

Spirituality: Power of the Believer 27

The School of *Tazkiyya*: The Qur'anic Science of Treating the Self 29

The Importance of Remembrance 32

Criticisms of Sufism 33

The Different Schools of Spirituality 34

The Struggle against the Self 35
The Heart as Key to Spiritual Improvement 37
Diseases of the Heart 38
The Seventeen Ruinous Traits 44
Principles of the School of Spiritual Education 47
Love of Allah and Fear of Allah 48
Emptiness and Sweetness 49
The Methods of Training and Purification of the Self 50

Conclusion 67
Appendix: What the Scholars of Islam Said about *Tasawwuf* 69
Glossary 77
Other Publications 83

About the Author

World-renowned religious scholar Shaykh Muhammad Hisham Kabbani is featured in the ground-breaking book published by Georgetown University, *The 500 Most Influential Muslims* in *the World*. For decades he has promoted traditional Islamic principles of peace, tolerance, love, compassion and brotherhood, while rigorously opposing extremism in all its forms. He hails from a respected family of traditional Islamic scholars, which includes the former head of the Association of Muslim Scholars of Lebanon and the present grand mufti (highest Islamic religious authority) of Lebanon.

Shaykh Kabbani is highly trained, both as a western scientist and as an Islamic scholar. He received a bachelor's degree in chemistry and later studied medicine. Under the instruction of Shaykh ʿAbdAllāh ad-Daghestani, upon whose personal notes this book is based, he holds a degree in Islamic Divine Law. Shaykh Muḥammad Nazim Adil al-Haqqani, world leader of the Naqshbandi-Haqqani Sufi Order, authorized him to teach and counsel students in Sufism.

In his long-standing endeavor to promote a better understanding of traditional Islam, in February 2010, Shaykh Kabbani hosted HRH Charles, the Prince of Wales at a cultural event at the revered Old Trafford Stadium in Manchester, U.K. He has hosted two international conferences in the U.S., and regional conferences on a host of issues that attracted moderate Muslim scholars from Asia, the Far East, Middle East, Africa, U.K. and Eastern Europe. His counsel is sought by journalists, academics, policymakers and government leaders.

For thirty years, Shaykh Kabbani has consistently promoted peaceful cooperation among people of all beliefs. Since the early 1990s, he has launched numerous endeavors to bring moderate Muslims into the mainstream. Often at great personal risk, he has been instrumental in awakening Muslim social consciousness regarding the religious duty to stand firm against extremism and terrorism, for the benefit of all. His bright, hopeful outlook, with a goal to honor and serve all humanity, has helped millions understand the difference between moderate mainstream Muslims and minority extremist sects.

In the United States, Shaykh Kabbani serves as Chairman, Islamic Supreme Council of America; Founder, Naqshbandi Sufi Order of America; Advisor, World Organization for Resource Development and Education; Chairman, As-*Sunnah* Foundation of America; Founder, *The Muslim Magazine*. In the United Kingdom, Shaykh Kabbani is an advisor to Sufi Muslim Council, which consults to the British government on public policy and social and religious issues.

Other titles by Shaykh Kabbani include: *The Benefits of Bismillah 'ir-Rahman 'ir-Raheem & Surat al-Fatihah* (2013), *The Importance of Prophet Muhammad in Our Daily Life* (2013), *The Hierarchy of Saints* (2013), *The Dome of Provisions* (2012), *Salawat of Tremendous Blessings* (2012, also in Turkish/Spanish), *The Heavenly Power of Divine Obedience and Gratitude* (2012), *The Sufilive Series* (2010-2012), *At the Feet of My Master* (2010, 2 vols.), *The Nine-fold Ascent* (2009), *Banquet for the Soul* (2008), *Illuminations* (2007), *Universe Rising* (2007), *Symphony of Remembrance* (2007), *A Spiritual Commentary on the Chapter of Sincerity* (2006), *The Sufi Science of Self-Realization* (Fons Vitae, 2005), *Keys to the Divine Kingdom* (2005), *Classical Islam and the Naqshbandi Sufi Order* (2004), *The Naqshbandi Sufi Tradition Guidebook* (2004), *The Approach of Armageddon? An Islamic Perspective* (2003), *Encyclopedia of Muḥammad's Women Companions and the Traditions They Related* (1998, with Dr. Laleh Bakhtiar), *Encyclopedia of Islamic Doctrine* (7 vols. 1998), *Angels Unveiled* (1996), *The Naqshbandi Sufi Way* (1995), and *Remembrance of God Liturgy of the Sufi Naqshbandi Masters* (1994).

Introduction

This book is based on a compilation of lectures by Shaykh Kabbani throughout the United States and in international venues. It includes a presentation on spiritual Islam to HRH Prince Charles of Wales and lectures given before the Vice President of Indonesia and at a conference in Malaysia that addressed the spiritual aspects of psychology.

While in most circumstances Naqshbandi Sufi masters do not read from a written text—rather speaking from inspiration—in order to accommodate academic norms and forms of presentation, Shaykh Kabbani has written these detailed lectures regarding Shari'ah and *Taṣawwuf* to accompany what he presented orally as inspired through his heart by his teacher, Shaykh Nazim Adil al-Haqqani.

In these talks, Shaykh Kabbani presents the traditional Islamic perspectives on a number of important issues of the day, focusing on the adaptability of classical Islam to the needs of the time, exigencies of social and cultural change, and the advent of new approaches and methodologies in a number of facets of life. At the same time, Shaykh Kabbani brings an unusual viewpoint to contemporary issues, relating them to aspects of the psyche and an individual's spiritual state, as well as the societal impact and relationships and their influence on observance of Divine Law.

Shaykh Kabbani presents complex issues in the light of potent relevant examples from modern-day science while simultaneously relating them to the traditional understanding of classical Islam and the normative practices and unparalleled perfection found in the example of Prophet Muhammad.

Publisher's Notes

This book is directed to those familiar with the Sufi Way; however, to accommodate lay readers unfamiliar with Sufi terminology and practices, we have provided English translations of Arabic texts and a comprehensive glossary. Where Arabic terms are crucial to the discussion, we have included transliteration and footnoted explanations. For readers familiar with Arabic and Islamic teachings, for further clarity please consult the cited sources.

The original material is based on transcripts of a series of holy gatherings that serve as conduits of heavenly guidance. The *ṣuḥbah,* a divinely inspired talk that conveys powerful energy that uplifts the soul, is delivered by the "shaykh," a highly trained spiritual guide. To present the authentic flavor of such rare teachings, great care was taken to preserve the speaking styles of both the author and the illustrious shaykhs upon whose notes this book is based. Please pray that our shortcomings are corrected.

Translations from Arabic to English pose unique challenges that we have tried our best to make understandable to Western readers. In addition, please note the worldwide cultural practice of not including the definite article "the," as in "the Prophet," which is a more intimate reference that appears occasionally throughout this work.

Quotes from the Holy Qur'an are offset with chapter and verse cited. The Holy Traditions of Prophet Muḥammad (*āḥadīth)* are offset and cited, in most cases. Historic dates are often referenced as "*Hijri*" and "A.H." (After *Hijri*), which is the commencement of the Islamic calendar, when Prophet Muḥammad migrated from Mecca to Madinah in 622 C.E. (Christian Era) to escape religious persecution and form his early nation. A reference calendar has also been provided.

Where gender-specific pronouns such as "he" and "him" are applied in a general sense, no discrimination is intended towards women, upon whom The Almighty bestowed great honor.

Islamic teachings are primarily based on four sources, in this order:

- **Holy Qur'an**: the holy book of divine revelation (God's Word) granted to Prophet Muḥammad. Reference to Holy Qur'an appears as "4:12," indicating "Chapter 4, Verse 12."
- ***Sunnah***: holy traditions of Prophet Muḥammad ﷺ; the systematic recording of his words and actions that comprise the *ḥadīth*. For fifteen

centuries, Islam has applied a strict, highly technical standard, rating each narration in terms of its authenticity and categorizing its "transmission." As this book is not highly technical, we simplified the reporting of *ḥadīth*, but included the narrator and source texts to support the discussion at hand.

- ***Ijma*'**: The adherence, or agreement of the experts of independent reasoning *(āhl al-ijtihād)* to the conclusions of a given ruling pertaining to what is permitted and what is forbidden after the passing of the Prophet, Peace be upon him, as well as the agreement of the Community of Muslims concerning what is obligatorily known of the religion with its decisive proofs. Perhaps a clearer statement of this principle is, "We do not separate (in belief and practice) from the largest group of the Muslims."
- **Legal Rulings:** highly trained Islamic scholars form legal rulings from their interpretation of the Qur'an and the *Sunnah*, known as *ijtihād.* Such rulings are intended to provide Muslims an Islamic context regarding contemporary social norms. In theological terms, scholars who form legal opinions have completed many years of rigorous training and possess degrees similar to a doctorate in divinity in Islamic knowledge, or in legal terms, hold the status of a high court or supreme court judge, or higher.

The following universally recognized symbols have been respectfully included in this work as they are deeply appreciated by a vast majority of our readers.

ﷻ *Subḥānahu wa Taʿalā* (may His Glory be Exalted), recited after the name "Allāh" and any of the Islamic names of God.

ﷺ *ṢallAllāhu ʿalayhi wa sallam* (God's blessings and greetings of peace be upon him), recited after the holy name of Prophet Muḥammad.

ؑ *ʿAlayhi ʿs-salām* (peace be upon him/her), recited after holy names of other prophets, names of Prophet Muḥammad's relatives, the pure and virtuous women in Islam, and angels.

ؓ/ؓ *RaḍīAllāhu ʿanh(um)* (may God be pleased with him/her), recited after the holy names of Companions of Prophet Muḥammad; plural, *raḍīAllāhu ʿanhum.*

ق represents *QaddasAllāhu sirrah* (may God sanctify his secret), recited after names of saints.

TRANSLITERATION

Transliteration from Arabic to English poses challenges. To show respect, Muslims often capitalize nouns that, in English, normally appear in lowercase.

To facilitate authentic pronunciation of names, places and terms, use the following key:

Symbol	Transliteration	Symbol	Transliteration	Vowels: Long	
ء	'	ط	ṭ	آ ى	
ب	b	ظ	ẓ	و	
ت	t	ع	'	ي	
ث	th	غ	gh	Short	
ج	j	ف	f	َ	
ح	ḥ	ق	q	ُ	
خ	kh	ك	k	ِ	
د	d	ل	l		
ذ	dh	م	m		
ر	r	ن	n		
ز	z	ه	h		
س	s	و	w		
ش	sh	ي	y		
ص	ṣ	ة	ah; at		
ض	ḍ	ال	al-/'l-		

THE SUFIS[1]

[1]Presented at the conference "Understanding Sufism and its Potential Role in US Policy", hosted by The Nixon Center, October 24, 2003.

Enlightened Community Builders

Sufism created community. In every age and era since the time of Prophet Muhammad, upon whom be peace, to whom all Sufis look as inspiration, role model and guide, the Sufis have sought to establish the infrastructure that, in modern parlance, would be termed privatized social welfare. It was through institutions designed not only to serve the destitute, the homeless and the ill, but whose overall purpose was to redirect the society as a whole to the goal of uplifting the people spiritually, psychologically, morally and physically, that the Sufis were able to have an immense impact on the societies in which they functioned.

The primary focus of the Sufi tradition was to establish societal order based on a hierarchical pattern of organization. Such a hierarchy governed Central Asia, South Asia, North Africa and most other areas of the Islamic world by means of Sufi societal infrastructure and institutions.

THE SUFI HIERARCHY

The primary mechanism by which Sufism exerted maximal societal impact was a sophisticated system of charities and trusts (*awqāf*). This pyramidal system was governed by a leader who directed these institutions to work to help those in most need first, followed by those at the next level of priority and so on, addressing the needs of all those in need, without leaving anyone outside the gambit of its programs. This paradigm was not dissimilar to contemporary modern day structured government-operated social programs (like public schools, hospitals, etc.) or civic society institutions. Leaders were chosen not by virtue of intelligence or political savvy, but solely by virtue of piety and wisdom, attained through disciplined participation in the Sufi school system.

The basic functional units of this infrastructure were the *khāniqah* (also known as *zāwīya* and *dargah*), buildings similar to modern hostels, but with far greater functionality and the *maljā* hospitals where all comers were treated without charge. *Khāniqahs* were places where people, both locals and travelers, could stay, eat, sleep and meet with one another. In addition to feeding and entertaining people, the institutions introduced them to Sufi customs.

Perhaps the closest parallel in westerns society to the Sufi system of societal welfare and the institutions it built would be found among the Catholic orders—particularly the Benedictine and Franciscan—many of which encountered Sufis during the Crusades and emulated them after they returned from Europe.

Unfortunately, the Wahhabis have destroyed this system of community-building. They closed the *khāniqahs* in order to eliminate the fundamental underlying principles of tolerance and openness upon which they were founded. Wahhabis sought to create a form of individualism that encouraged Muslims to reinterpret their religion according to their own whims, thereby undermining the traditional Sufi hierarchy. The result was a sort of individualistic anarchy that found differences in the most trivial aspects of religion, culture or lifestyle to be wholly unacceptable and grounds for often fierce and bitter clashes. Whenever the hierarchy established by Sufism was dismantled, disorder, confusion and anarchy took its place with inevitable result being division, destructive enmity and a downward spiral into violence.

THE SUFI APPROACH TO ADVANCEMENT

Sufism was based on the fundamental importance of the relationship between student and teacher. In Sufism, the top of the pyramid is only reached by means of education and experience. Like any important job, it requires an intensive period of internship (much as is required to become a public servant, a doctor or a lawyer). This approach to training future leaders builds integrity and relies on the test of time to confirm true leaders, those who possess insight, wisdom and divine guidance. Sufi teachings focused on the importance of self-sacrifice and the need for those well-endowed to share from what God had graced them with, whether in material wealth, learning or piety.

Sufism eliminated the anarchy of self-centeredness and cooled the rebellion of desire and egoism, enabling the accomplished Sufi to lead others. The result of this disciplined practical training was that esteemed Sufi figures were historically well accomplished in the sciences of Islamic spirituality.

PRINCIPLES OF TREATING THE SELF

Islamic spirituality calls for *zuhd* (asceticism), *war'a* (sincerity) and *riḍā* (acceptance of the divine decree of one's allotted share). The Sufi belief is that reason alone is not sufficient to make decisions; they believe it is also essential to understand the underlying reality of each issue one faces. To understand such realities, one must undergo physical and spiritual training exercises, much as a wrestler must do weight training and wind-sprints, in order to prevent the anarchy and corrupt desire of the self from controlling one in the state of anger, lust or fear. Once this training is successfully accomplished, passions at the basest level will no longer control one; rather, one will control them. When this has been accomplished, decisions will no longer be based on egoism, anger or selfishness, but will be based on reason, intellect and wisdom, informed by spiritual inspiration.

To the Sufis, the whole world is in their hands, and at the same time, their hearts are in the hand of their Creator, for they observe the maxim of the Prophet's Companion, 'Alī who said:

اعمل لدنياك كأنك تعيش ابدا واعمل لآخرتك كأنك تموت غدا

Work for this life as if you were going to live forever, but work for the Afterlife as if you were going to die today.

The utmost level of submission for the Sufi, and the ultimate attainment, is to "die before you die," meaning that one's heart is no longer attached to the material world, but is directed to the Divine Presence, seeking God's good pleasure, always striving to serve humanity in every possible way. Such idealism and detachment sounds almost impossible to achieve humanly, but in fact, this was achieved by countless numbers of people who flocked to the doors of the Sufi shaykhs in their retreats and hostels and trained their selves with determination and discipline.

Sufis say that a human being can be rich and ascetic at the same time, for to be ascetic, one need not be poor. Not every poor one is an ascetic, nor is every ascetic one poor. For this reason, history shows many Sufi saints were, in fact, quite wealthy, but spent their wealth in God's Way by aiding the needy, building hostels, hospitals and way stations, and by establishing trusts to promote the arts, libraries and scientific research centers.

The Sufis say, "The wise servants of God are like the Earth. They accept every type of refuse to be cast upon them and yet nothing issues from them but sweetness. Both the righteous and the sinner walk upon it." The Earth is characterized by strength. Whatever God Wills, the Earth accepts. It has no will of its own. In this respect, the Sufis resemble the Earth in that "every vile and ugly thing is cast upon" then, and they accept it. Yet, after the Sufi accepts to be such a dump, the verse continues, "nothing comes from him or her except goodness."

Such wise teachers do not treat you the same way that you treat them. Rather, they return good for evil. By this means, a counterforce comes into play by which the momentum of evil, passing through the transformative positive energy field of the advanced Sufi master, is converted into power that is rebounded to the opponent, causing a catalytic reaction that inverts the initial impulse to evil, resulting in a transfiguration of the challenger. For that reason, some of the most famous conversions in Islam came about when an opponent sought out a Sufi master seeking to harm him, yet when confronted with his own evil in the Sufi's mirror-like visage, was thus brought to contrition, repentance and redemption at the hands of the master.

THE DOCTORS OF HEARTS

With the knowledge acquired through their sincerity and piety, Sufis were able to first treat their own hearts. From this experience of self-treatment, they began to understand the illnesses of others. Through their immersion in the social life of their communities, they empathized with the feelings of pain others felt and sought the means to cure their spiritual, moral, psychological and social ills. With the wisdom and experience acquired in treating their own ills, using their understanding of culture and environment and maintaining the flexibility to accommodate the lives of all sorts of people, the Sufi leaders and healers were able to treat the people in whatever situation they found them.

Sufism is not words put together in flashy phrases, nor is it theoretical knowledge; rather, it is moral character and behavior, it is the state of excellence, and it is the infrastructure of life. One of Sufism's greatest scholars, al-Junayd, said:

"We did not take *Taṣawwuf* from 'this one said' or 'that one said,' as the scholars did [with their *sanads*, chains of transmission and verification], but we took it by feeling the hunger of the hungry, by feeling abandoned in the desert with the homeless, by feeling the wealth of the rich in accompanying them, by feeling the pain of the ill, by feeling the pain of the injured. That is how we came to this understanding."

Thus, *Taṣawwuf* was never based on theories to be mentioned and discussed, nor on a prescription to be taken from a pharmacy. Rather *Taṣawwuf* provided a cure first tested by the doctor on himself who, after successfully deriving its benefit, was able to apply it to others in need of the same treatment. This is what made the central social role of Sufism in Muslim life acceptable to the masses, wherever it was found.

The way of the Sufi Path was one of transformation, as symbolized by the alchemical metaphor of transforming base elements, such as lead, into gold. This path of continual transformation resulted in a constant struggle to not only elevate the spiritual level of the individual, but also to raise the spiritual and material levels of the family, the tribe, the community and the nation as a whole. The French scholar Louis Massignon explains that social justice remained crucial to the ascetics' piety: "The mystic call is, as a rule, the result of inner rebellion of the conscience against social injustices, not only those of others, but primarily and particularly, against one's own faults ...."

Sufis had, and continue to play, a great role in social work, as is mentioned by Massignon and many other Orientalists. As the former stated, "The Sufis are doctors of the soul, [whose work] includes the sociology of the soul, the psychology of the soul and the mentality of the soul, and they work to cure those who have diseases in any of these aspects."[2]

THE SUFI APPROACH TO SOCIETY-BUILDING

Sufis worked to build bridges of inter-racial, inter-ethnic and cross-cultural understanding. In doing so, they differed from the Wahhabis, who tried to

[2]Massignon, Louis, *Les origines du lexique technique de la mystique mussulmanes*, p. 16, Paris, 1954

homogenize, standardize and eliminate all variation, in contradiction with the Qur'ānic verse:

يَا أَيُّهَا النَّاسُ إِنَّا خَلَقْنَاكُم مِّن ذَكَرٍ وَأُنثَى وَجَعَلْنَاكُمْ شُعُوبًا وَقَبَائِلَ لِتَعَارَفُوا إِنَّ أَكْرَكُمْ عِندَ اللهِ أَتْقَاكُمْ
إِنَّ اللهَ عَلِيمٌ خَبِيرٌ

O Mankind! We created you from a single (pair) of a male and a female, and made you into nations and tribes, that you may know each other (not that you may despise (each other).[3]

As an example of this spirit, sacred education, community-building and human resource development was spread throughout Africa by the Sufi orders, creating jobs for the poor and establishing relationships between disparate communities. Especially active in such social work were the Shaḍiliyya and the Sanusiyya orders. The hostels founded by the shaykhs of these Sufi orders became points of convergence, bringing together different races, promoting interracial and inter-tribal marriages, and thereby, preventing wars and creating intellectual and economic opportunities for the societies in which they functioned by introducing science, business, trade, education, medicine, the arts and administrative job opportunities for people. This was accomplished by the mixing of the highly accomplished and revered Sufi teachers with the common people, the normative practice of the Sufis. To involve themselves in the lives of the common people both rich and poor without any thought to distinctions of ethnicity, culture or even religion, rather, considering all people members of the same human community, had an enormous impact on cultures and tribes previously isolated from, or more commonly, at war with each other.

Sufism depended on the human bonding that comes about with the commingling of peoples in a symbiotic manner, producing combinations that cut across a society's natural barriers, to generate the heat and turbulence needed to keep a nourishing flow of social "nutrients" moving among all the layers and stratum that make up a healthy human community. It was this tremendous spirit of egalitarianism and leveling that endeared the Sufi leaders, the *shuyukh* (literally "wise ones" or "elders"), to both the common people and the elite alike, enabling them to act as catalysts

---

[3]Sūratu 'l-Ḥujurāt [The Private Apartments], 49:13.

for interaction and the building of social ties in otherwise polarized and factionalized societies. This was in keeping with the tradition of the Prophet Muhammad who, upon his emigration to Medina, built the "model city," in which Jews, Christians, Muslims, Zoroastrians and idol-worshippers were able to live together in a spirit of goodness, tolerance and cooperation, a reality not unlike that of modern, democratic societies.

SUFISM AND RELIGIOUS PLURALITY

Taṣawwuf, which is the essence of the true religious tradition of Prophet Muhammad and is distinguished by his high humanistic principles, is open to all religions and races. By nature, Islam is a religion open to peoples of every race. It does not differentiate between one Muslim and another. The Sufis have stretched the bounds of this principle to the point where they do not even see any difference between their religion and other faiths. They opened their doors to accept all other religions without distinction.

The Sufis call to all people, just as God sends His Mercy to all humanity, without distinguishing between those who believe in His Existence and those who do not. The renowned Naqshbandi Sufi saint Bayazid al-Bistami said, "Sufis, in general, seek God's mercy for everyone, not solely for Muslims."

In another of his famous ecstatic utterances, Bayazid, on passing a Jewish cemetery, exclaimed, "They are excused (*mādhurūn*)." What he meant here was, "O God, these people must be destined for Paradise, because they are Your creation and they did not know your last Prophet." As he passed a Muslim cemetery, he observed, "They are proud and arrogant (*maghrūrūn)* in believing they are going to Paradise and everyone else is destined for Hellfire."

Another outstanding Sufi master of the thirteenth century, Jalaluddin Rumi said, "O Muslims, what do I have to say? I do not know myself whether I am a Christian, a Jew, a Zoroastrian or a Muslim. And I do not know myself if I am eastern or western, upper or lower. And I do not know myself if I am from Earth or I am from on high. And I do not know myself if I am Indian, Chinese, Bulgarian, Iraqi or Khorasani. I do not know myself if I even have an appearance or not, whether I have existence or not, if have a location or not. I do not know myself if I am a body or a soul. But what I do know is that my soul is the soul of souls. When I put my name with my

Lord's, I saw the universe as one. I see One, I sing One, I know One and I read One."[4]

In his poetry, the great Sufi Ibn al-Fārid shows the commonality between all religions based on his experience with Christians, Jews, Brahmins and Muslims. He says, "I see in all of them the divisions of one fountain, and it is the attainment of the eye of sincerity to see them all as equal."

This is how the Sufi Muslims, through their rarefied understanding of the nature of society emerged as the fountainheads of religious and moral character. This was because of their openness to all different experiences in religion and human philosophy, and their harmonizing with all other spiritual influences and backgrounds, coming altogether under the perfect human university, bringing the diverse elements of society together under the commonality of the human experience without regard for the differences of culture and the happenstances of geography.

Nicholson observed, "*Taṣawwuf* is a combination and adaptation of different philosophies and beliefs by means of which Islamic spirituality was disseminated."

The great Orientalist scholar Martin Lings said, "I am European and yet I found the safety of my soul in *Taṣawwuf*."

EMPHASIS ON ART

Through the Sufi emphasis on the figurative, art became a metaphor for the Path to the Divine, and in its various forms took on a life of their own, expressing the yearning of the seeker, the satisfaction of the benign self, and the passion of the lovers. Poetry, an art form dear to the early Arab Muslims, grew into a particularly potent vehicle for expressing the Sufi devotions. Sufism's social calling found expression in the sciences, particularly in alchemy, astronomy and in seeking to heal, through medicine, massage and natural healing methods.

---

[4]Shams Tabriz, *Diwan*, (translated by R. A. Nicholson), p. 344.

As with all things, the openness of the Sufis allowed the variety and diversity of the many cultures it encountered to enter, expand and decorate the expressions of Sufi art and works of social welfare. Similarly, in the field of philosophy and intellect, the teachings of Plato, Aristotle, the Jewish sages, the Zoroastrians and the Buddhists all found a "second home" within the Sufi camp. It was in this spirit of acceptance that an eclectic milieu emerged that allowed individuality to flourish while, at the same time and under the careful guidance and wisdom of the Sufi masters, maintaining society's focus on a common, final goal.

Sufis emphasized poetry, lyrics, music, songs and chanting of many different kinds and in many different dialects. The blending of all these different dialects created even more interrelationships between communities. Thus, it is not uncommon even today to find Javanese Sufis chanting praises of the Prophet in a Yemeni dialect of Arabic, or Sufis in Afghanistan reciting Turkish poetry of love of God.

INNER PEACE, OUTER DIALOGUE

It was the emphasis on the internal struggle to purify the self of one's innermost dark characteristics that made the Sufis the foremost callers to peace. Sufis used diplomacy and wisdom to building bridges between their enemies by means of education and negotiation, rather than resorting to conflict and force of arms.

SUFISM AND THE PERENNIAL CONFLICT OF GOOD AND EVIL[5]

[5]Presented at the International Seminar on Spiritual Psychology, University of Malaya, Kuala Lumpur, Malaysia, August 23, 2007.

Abstract

Evil has been a problem for Mankind since the advent of the first humans on Earth. Cain killed his own brother, Abel, so that his ritual sacrifice might seem more worthy in the eyes of Allah, proof that the outward forms of religiosity are not sufficient to check the negative traits of the lower self. More is required to purify the self from these evil impulses. Abel had developed this quality, as evidenced by his refusal to harm his brother even when faced with the threat of death. His was the state of purified spiritual character. That character is not developed in a vacuum, but requires a focused discipline to achieve. It is a discipline that was developed and refined by subsequent generations into a systematic path of self-analysis and self-correction that became known as the "Science of the Self," or Sufism.

Sufi discipline has always played an essential role in the life of human beings. It builds upon the teachings of scholars and spiritual scientists imbued with wisdom, sagacity and the courage to stand for what is right. Such teachers were intellectually adept, able to appeal not only to the masses but to academics and people of import.

Psychologically, Sufism works to neutralize the caustic character of negative personality traits, just as a base in a chemical reaction counters the properties of an acid. The wise men and women who have mastered this path are able purify themselves in this life are able to neutralize the axes of evil that so often seek to dominate human discourse.

Introduction

The struggle between good and evil is a perennial conflict that has been ongoing throughout human history. It has been unfolding from the time of the first man and woman, Adam ﵇ and Eve, as evidenced by the dramatic showdown between their two children, Abel and Cain.[6]

Abel, who represented good, was always in conflict with his brother, Cain, who represented evil. Both sought to worship Allah ﷻ, and both were asked to render a sacrifice. However, under the influence of Satan, Cain chose as his gift the worst, most diseased sheep in his flock. Abel presented his best yearling. Abel's sacrifice was accepted, but Cain's was rejected. Out of overwhelming envy, Cain slew Abel.

Regarding this, Allah ﷻ says:

وَاتْلُ عَلَيْهِمْ نَبَأَ ابْنَيْ آدَمَ بِالْحَقِّ إِذْ قَرَّبَا قُرْبَانًا فَتُقُبِّلَ مِنْ أَحَدِهِمَا وَلَمْ يُتَقَبَّلْ مِنَ الْآخَرِ
قَالَ لَأَقْتُلَنَّكَ قَالَ إِنَّمَا يَتَقَبَّلُ اللَّهُ مِنَ الْمُتَّقِينَ

And convey unto them, setting forth the truth, the story of the two sons of Adam, how each offered a sacrifice and it was accepted from one of them, whereas it was not accepted from the other. [And Cain] said: "I will surely slay you!" [Abel] replied: "Behold, Allah accepts only from those who are conscious of Him. Even if you lay your hand on me to slay me, I shall not lay my hand on you to slay you! Behold, I fear Allah, the Sustainer of All the Worlds."[i]

Through this one sees Abel's purity of heart and his tolerance for his brother. More importantly, it shows his acceptance. Acceptance is a profound concept, because it goes far beyond mere tolerance. When we say we tolerate someone, we mean that we put up with his shortcomings and faults. To accept someone is to acknowledge his right to be himself, withholding both judgment and criticism. It represents a higher state of submission to Divine Will and issues from a place of unconditional love, making it a rare quality indeed.

---

[6] Hābīl and Qābīl.

Allah ﷻ gave every person the right to defend himself from harm, but Abel adhered to an even higher standard. He said, "I am not extending my hand and I am not even defending myself." Here again, we see another example of utter submission to his Lord and acceptance of His Divine Will.

Abel was motivated by the same high level of faith that guided Sayyidina Ibrāhīm ﷺ when he was cast into the fire by Nimrod. Jibrīl ﷺ came and asked Ibrāhīm ﷺ if he needed help. His reply was, "No, for truly Allah ﷻ is seeing me and will give me what I need." He was not mistaken, for Allah ﷻ then said:

قُلْنَا يَا نَارُ كُونِي بَرْدًا وَسَلَامًا عَلَىٰ إِبْرَاهِيمَ

We said, "O Fire! Be you cool on Ibrāhīm"[7]

In this tremendous trial, Sayyidina Ibrāhīm ﷺ showed the highest level of submission to Allah ﷻ, for even though he recognized Jibrīl ﷺ as Allah's ﷻ messenger to the prophets, he said, "The one sending you knows what I need. I seek whatever He Wills." If Jibrīl ﷺ had said, "Allah ﷻ is sending me to ensure that you are safe," then Sayyidina Ibrāhīm ﷺ would have accepted. There is tremendous subtlety in this affirmation of *tawḥīd*, for keep in mind, this all occurred in the course of a great physical struggle between good and evil: the conflict between Sayyidina Ibrāhīm ﷺ and Nimrod, who was the representative of Satan. Here, too, is another example of that perennial struggle.

GOAL OF THE BELIEVER: PERFECTION OF DIVINE SERVICE

Today, many Muslims believe that the purpose of Islam is to take them to Paradise and save them from Hell. In reality, this is only a secondary goal.

وَمَا خَلَقْتُ الْجِنَّ وَالْإِنسَ إِلَّا لِيَعْبُدُونِ

I have only created jinns and men, that they may worship Me.[8]

---

[7]Sūratu'l-Anbīyā [The Prophets], 21:69.
[8]Sūratu 'dh-Dhāriyāt [The Winnowing Winds], 51:56.

Muhammad al-Asad, in his commentary on this verse, states:

Thus, the innermost purpose of the creation of all rational beings is their cognition (*maʿrifah*) of the existence of Allah and, hence, their conscious willingness to conform their own existence to whatever they may perceive of His will and plan: and it is this twofold concept of cognition and willingness that gives the deepest meaning to what the Qur'ān describes as "worship" (*ʿibādah*). As the next verse shows, this spiritual call does not arise from any supposed "need" on the part of the Creator, who is self-sufficient and infinite in His power, but is designed as an instrument for the inner development of the worshipper, who, by the act of his conscious self-surrender to the all-pervading Creative Will, may hope to come closer to an understanding of that Will and, thus, closer to Allah Himself.

Sayyidina ʿAlī ﷺ said:

All goodness is found in four character traits: Aṣ-ṣamt, knowing when to keep silent; an-nuṭaq, awareness of what you speak; an-naẓr, awareness of what you observe; and al-ḥaraka, awareness of where you are moving.

And he said:

Every speech, if it is not in dhikrullāh, is considered laghaw, idle talk, of no importance. And every silence not in thinking and meditating on Allah ﷻ is considered heedlessness. And everything observed by the eyes from which one does not take an example is heedlessness. And every movement not in taʿabudun, worship, is useless, faṭara. May Your Mercy envelop someone who made his speech Your Remembrance (nuṭuqdhikruk) and made his silence contemplation and remembrance, and made his vision an example and made his movements worship. By that way the person will be saved from his tongue and his hand. [9]

From these examples, we see that Mankind was created to worship Allah ﷻ. The Prophet ﷺ came to teach us how to accomplish that fundamental purpose.

---

[9]*Kitāb al-lamaʿ*, p. 182.

WHAT THE PROPHET BROUGHT

Allah ﷻ sent Islam for all time:

إِنَّ الدِّينَ عِندَ اللَّهِ الْإِسْلَامُ

The Religion before Allah is Islam.[10]

هُوَ الَّذِي أَرْسَلَ رَسُولَهُ بِالْهُدَىٰ وَدِينِ الْحَقِّ لِيُظْهِرَهُ عَلَى الدِّينِ كُلِّهِ وَلَوْ كَرِهَ الْمُشْرِكُونَ

It is He Who hath sent His Messenger with guidance and the Religion of Truth, to proclaim it over all religion, even though the Pagans may detest (it).[11]

Islam consists of two aspects: belief and practice. Its purpose is to take each individual Muslim on a personal journey towards Allah ﷻ, while at the same time creating a community in which people live together and work together as servants of Allah ﷻ, striving to establish an ideal society, living under His guidance and seeking ongoing improvement and steadfast observance of Allah's religion.

Living the religion of Islam depends on practices and actions. In the process of that journey, we face ongoing struggles between our instincts, egoistic desires and carnal lusts on the one hand, and the divine principles and good manners that the religion calls us to on the other. This struggle is continuous and like a war, in that victory or defeat are taking place at every moment. Evil may overcome the good for a time, and then good may overcome evil. Ultimately, one side overwhelms the other. The hope is that good will prevail. When the power of good surpasses that of evil, the individual soul begins to ascend through levels of knowledge that enables its possessor to prevent the ego's selfish mastery. This enables the seeker to fully comply with and fulfill Allah's Orders with alacrity. This is experienced on the seeker's journey as manifestations of virtue emerging on the horizon of the self.

The struggle, however, is long. We are torn by truth and falsehood, greed and generosity, happiness and regret, pulled towards Heaven, then

---

[10]Sūrat Āli-'Imrān [The Family of 'Imrān], 3:19.
[11]Sūratu 't-Tawbah [Repentance], 9:33.

goaded towards Hellfire. The only way to avoid that bad ending is to override our selfishness, our egoistic desires and our carnal lusts. Such a victory can only come through faith, *Īmān*. Allah ﷻ sent the Prophet Muhammad ﷺ so that we might acquire this important trait, and thus advance on our spiritual journey towards Him.

Allah ﷻ said:

هُوَ الَّذِي بَعَثَ فِي الْأُمِّيِّينَ رَسُولًا مِّنْهُمْ يَتْلُو عَلَيْهِمْ آيَاتِهِ وَيُزَكِّيهِمْ وَيُعَلِّمُهُمُ الْكِتَابَ وَالْحِكْمَةَ وَإِن كَانُوا مِن قَبْلُ لَفِي ضَلَالٍ مُّبِينٍ

It is He Who has sent amongst the Unlettered an apostle from among themselves, to recite unto them His revelations, to purify them, and to instruct them in the Book and Wisdom, although they had been, before, in manifest error. [12]

Here Allah ﷻ makes clear that Sayyidina Muhammad's mission is first to teach revelation, then to purify us, then to teach us the Holy Qur'ān and wisdom. Note that *Tazkīyyat an-Nafs*, Purification of the Self, precedes learning the Holy Qur'ān and wisdom.

UMM AL-AHADITH: THE HADITH OF JIBRIL

We cite here the well-known *ḥadīth* of Jibrīl عليه السلام, which all scholars recognize as the source of the *Sunnah* and the source of all *ḥadīth* (*Umm as-Sunnah wa umm al-aḥādīth*). As one of the most important *ḥadīths* in Islam, it needs no additional support:

قَالَ حَدَّثَنِي اَبِي عُمَرُ بْنُ الْخَطَّابِ قَالَ بَيْنَمَا نَحْنُ عِنْدَ رَسُولِ اللهِّ صلى الله عليه وسلم ذَاتَ يَوْمٍ اِذْ طَلَعَ عَلَيْنَا رَجُلٌ شَدِيدُ بَيَاضِ الثِّيَابِ شَدِيدُ سَوَادِ الشَّعَرِ لاَ يُرَى عَلَيْهِ اَثَرُ السَّفَرِ وَلاَ يَعْرِفُهُ مِنَّا اَحَدٌ حَتَّى جَلَسَ اِلَى النَّبِيِّ صلى الله عليه وسلم فَاَسْنَدَ رُكْبَتَيْهِ اِلَى رُكْبَتَيْهِ وَوَضَعَ كَفَّيْهِ عَلَى فَخِذَيْهِ وَقَالَ يَا مُحَمَّدُ اَخْبِرْنِي عَنِ الإِسْلاَمِ . فَقَالَ رَسُولُ اللهَّ صلى الله عليه وسلم " الإِسْلاَمُ اَنْ تَشْهَدَ اَنْ لاَ اِلَهَ اِلاَّ اللهُ وَاَنَّ مُحَمَّدًا رَسُولُ اللهَّ وَتُقِيمَ الصَّلاَةَ وَتُؤْتِيَ الزَّكَاةَ وَتَصُومَ رَمَضَانَ وَتَحُجَّ الْبَيْتَ اِنِ اسْتَطَعْتَ اِلَيْهِ سَبِيلاً . قَالَ صَدَقْتَ . قَالَ فَعَجِبْنَا لَهُ يَسْاَلُهُ وَيُصَدِّقُهُ . قَالَ فَاَخْبِرْنِي عَنِ الإِيمَانِ . قَالَ " اَنْ تُؤْمِنَ بِاللهَّ وَمَلاَئِكَتِهِ وَكُتُبِهِ وَرُسُلِهِ وَالْيَوْمِ الآخِرِ وَتُؤْمِنَ بِالْقَدَرِ خَيْرِهِ وَشَرِّهِ " . قَالَ

---

[12]Sūratu 'l-Jumu'ah [Congregational Prayer], 62:2.2.

صَدَقْتَ . قَالَ فَاَخْبِرْنِي عَنِ الإِحْسَانِ . قَالَ " اَنْ تَعْبُدَ اللهَ كَاَنَّكَ تَرَاهُ فَاِنْ لَمْ تَكُنْ
تَرَاهُ فَاِنَّهُ يَرَاكَ " . قَالَ فَاَخْبِرْنِي عَنِ السَّاعَةِ . قَالَ " مَا الْمَسْئُولُ عَنْهَا بِاَعْلَمَ مِنَ السَّائِلِ " . قَالَ
فَاَخْبِرْنِي عَنْ اَمَارَتِهَا . قَالَ " اَنْ تَلِدَ الأَمَةُ رَبَّتَهَا وَاَنْ تَرَى الْحُفَاةَ
الْعُرَاةَ الْعَالَةَ رِعَاءَ الشَّاءِ يَتَطَاوَلُونَ فِي الْبُنْيَانِ " . قَالَ ثُمَّ انْطَلَقَ فَلَبِثْتُ مَلِيًّا ثُمَّ قَالَ لِي " يَا عُمَرُ اَتَدْرِي
مَنِ السَّائِلُ " . قُلْتُ اللهُ وَرَسُولُهُ اَعْلَمُ . قَالَ " فَاِنَّهُ جِبْرِيلُ
اَتَاكُمْ يُعَلِّمُكُمْ دِينَكُمْ

From ʿUmar ﵁ who said, "While we were one day sitting with the Messenger of Allah ﷺ, there appeared before us a man with a very white garment, and very black hair. No traces of journeying were visible on him and none of us knew him. He sat down close by the Prophet ﷺ, rested his knees against his and put his palms on his thighs and said, 'O Muhammad inform me about Islam.' Said the Messenger ﷺ: 'Islam is that you should testify that there is no deity save Allah and that Muhammad is His Messenger, that you should say the prayers, pay the zakāt, fast during Ramadan and go on Hajj to the House if you can find a way to do so.' He said, 'You have spoken truly.' We were astonished at his first questioning him and telling him that he was right, but he went on to say: 'Inform me about Īmān.' Muhammad ﷺ answered: 'It is that you believe in Allah and His angels, and his books and his messengers and in the last Day and that you should believe in the Decreeing of both good and evil.' He said: 'You have spoken truly.' Then he said: 'Inform me about Iḥsān [perfection of character].' The Messenger answered: 'It is that you should serve Allah as though you could see Him, for though you cannot see Him, yet He sees you.'...Thereupon the man went off. I waited a while and then the Prophet ﷺ said: 'O ʿUmar do you know who that was?' I replied: 'Allah and His Messenger know better.' He said: 'That was Jibrīl. He came to teach you your religion.'"[13]

In this *ḥādīth*, the archangel Jibrīl ﵇ divided religion into three categories or main branches, from which everything else, all *aḥadıth* and all *Sunnah*, flows. He also emphasized the divisions between each branch by asking about each one separately.

The first is Islam, the practical side of the religion that includes worship, deeds and other obligations. It relates to the external aspect of the

[13]Bukhārī and Muslim.

self, the body and the community. Scholars call this Shariʿah. It is the subject of *ʿIlm al-Fiqh,* the Science of Jurisprudence.

THE SECOND COMPONENT OF *DIN AL-ISLAM*: *IMAN* (BELIEF)

The second category, *Imān,* is the expression of belief through the mind and heart. This means belief in Allah ﷻ, His Messengers, His Books, the Angels, the Last Day, and Destiny. This became known to scholars as *ʿIlm at-Tawḥīd,* the Science of Divine Unity, or *ʿIlm al-ʿAqā'id,* the Science of Doctrine.

The meaning of *Imān* is elaborated on elsewhere in the Holy Qur'ān:

قَالَتِ الْأَعْرَابُ آمَنَّا قُل لَّمْ تُؤْمِنُوا وَلَكِن قُولُوا أَسْلَمْنَا وَلَمَّا يَدْخُلِ الْإِيمَانُ فِي قُلُوبِكُمْ وَإِن تُطِيعُوا اللَّهَ
وَرَسُولَهُ لَا يَلِتْكُم مِّنْ أَعْمَالِكُمْ شَيْئًا إِنَّ اللَّهَ غَفُورٌ رَّحِيمٌ

The desert Arabs say, "We believe." Say, "Ye have no faith; but you (only) say, 'We have submitted our wills to Allah,' For not yet has Faith entered your hearts. But if you obey Allah and His Messenger, He will not belittle aught of your deeds: for Allah is Oft-Forgiving, Most Merciful."[14]

Here, Allah ﷻ informs the desert Arabs that they have yet to attain true belief. Rather, they have achieved the level of Islam. They became Muslims, but faith did not yet enter their hearts. Faith entails belief in the Unseen, *al-Imān bi'l-Ghayb,* and the highest level of faith is to testify to the truth of the Prophet's statements, as Sayyidina Abū Bakr did when the Quraysh confronted him saying, "Your companion claims to have ascended to Heaven and returned in one night. What do you say to that?" and he replied, "The Messenger of Allah spoke the truth."

THE THIRD COMPONENT OF DIN AL-ISLAM: IHSAN (PERFECTION OF CHARACTER)

The third aspect of religion is known as *Iḥsān,* Perfection of Character. It combines the first category, worship, and the second, belief, to reach the State of Presence. This is why the *Maqām al-Iḥsān* is described as worshipping Allah ﷻ "as if you are seeing Him." The qualifier "as if" is

---

[14]Sūratu 'l-Ḥujurāt [The Private Apartments], 49:14.

necessary, because in reality we cannot see Allah ﷻ. However, we can reach a level where we realize that Allah ﷻ is seeing us. That is a colossal perception, and it is sometimes termed *al-yaqīn*, certainty. One who has reached this state of perception is granted a taste of spiritual pleasure and illuminated with the light of knowledge by Allah ﷻ. The heart of the seeker is filled with His Favors and Grants.

The path to this high station of spiritual awareness has been termed by scholars the Science of Truth, *'Ilm al-Ḥaqīqat*. In the time nearest to the Prophet ﷺ, during the lives of the Ṣaḥāba, it was known as *"aṣ-Ṣiddiqīyya"*, the path of the veracious. Later, it become known as *'Ilm at-Taṣawwuf*, the Science of Sufism.

We see then that Islam prescribes the behavior of a Muslim, *Īmān* relates to his beliefs and defines them, and *Iḥsān* refers to the state of the heart that determines whether his Islam and *Iḥsān* will bear fruit in this life and the Next.

THE RELATIONSHIP BETWEEN SHARI'AH AND *HAQIQAT*

Understanding the distinctions that separate these three components of religion, we can then turn to the relationship between *Fiqh*, the science of jurisprudence, and *Taṣawwuf*, the science of *Iḥsān*. To understand this relationship, it is useful to consider the example of prayer.

The science of *fiqh* teaches us that we must perform our prayer in full accordance with the rules of the Shariʿah, including all of the prescribed actions, invocations and intentions. This is known as *jassad aṣ-ṣalāt*, the body of the prayer. Included in these is the requirement to keep the heart in Allah's Divine Presence and to know that Allah is observing you during the entire prayer. The external form of the *ṣalāt* is its body, and the humility and self-effacement, *khushu*ʿ, is its soul, or *ruḥ*. This is the essence of the prayer, but we know from our own experience that people sometimes perform the outward actions of *ṣalāt* without this inner awareness in their hearts. The one who performs the outward actions of *ṣalāt* without maintaining this awareness of the Divine Presence is like a zombie.

As the soul needs the body in which to live, so too does the body need the soul to give it life. The proper relationship between Shariʿah and *Ḥaqīqat* is like the relationship between body and soul. The perfect believer who has reached the state of *Iḥsān* is the one who can conjoin Shariʿah and *Ḥaqīqat*.

That is why *Imān* came directly after the Five Pillars of Islam in *Umm al-Ḥadīth* that defined *al-aqāʿid,* the doctrine of Islam. If *Imān* is strong, then one can ascend to the third level, which is moral excellence, the state of *Iḥsān. Imān* is the mindset of belief, *ʿitiqādfikrī. Imān* is a theoretical belief that requires strong character to accept. *Imān* needs a booster. That booster is the spiritual dimension of the self.

Returning to the story of Cain and Abel, we see now that Cain was arrogant and his faith was weak. These diseases of the heart led him to kill his brother and lie to his Lord. He fulfilled Allah's Order to make a sacrifice, but his intention was impure. His story is important, for it shows us that one can perform the outward acts required by the religion and still fail to fulfill the attending obligations because those actions lack sincerity and are, therefore, not accepted.

Consider the case of one who performs his obligatory prayers, but while doing so conspires in his mind against his brother or sister. Will his prayer be accepted? A Muslim who prays and fasts but does not have a purified soul and does not have a *qalbun dhākiran,* heart that remembers Allah ﷻ, but who instead gives himself over to all kinds of pleasures and desires, one who never knew humbleness, sincerity, or struggles in the Way of Allah, his heart is dead although he performs his prayers. He is a Muslim in appearance, but not in reality. What is the benefit of a dry prayer that has no soul in it and no life? In such a person Islam becomes weak and faith becomes weak because there is no warmth, no *shawk,* no love, no yearning, no emotion, no fear, no compassion. That one is no different from someone who is not a Muslim.

وعن أبي هريرة قال قال رسول الله صلى الله عليه وسلم (آية المنافق ثلاث . إذا حدث كذب وإذا وعد أخلف وإذا اؤتمن خان وإن صام وصلى وزعم أنه مسلم . (مسلم)

Abū Hurayrah ؓ *narrated that the Prophet* ﷺ *said, "A hypocrite has three distinguishing signs; first when he talks he lies; when he makes a promise he breaks it; and when something is entrusted to him he misappropriates it. And [this is the case] even if he prays and fasts and considers himself a Muslim."* [15]

---

[15] Bukhārī and Muslim.

How many Muslims today observe all five pillars, yet when they speak they lie; when they make business deals they cheat and when they enter politics they are deceitful. Such people make promises they do not keep, and they feel no remorse in eating the money of other Muslims. Such a person, even if he offers the prayers and keeps the fast, and considers himself a pious mosque-attendee, is still a hypocrite.

عَنْ سَهْلِ بْنِ سَعْدٍ السَّاعِدِيِّ،أَنَّهُ قَالَ مَرَّ رَجُلٌ عَلَى رَسُولِ اللّٰهِ صلى الله عليه وسلم فَقَالَ لِرَجُلٍ عِنْدَهُ جَالِسٍ " مَا رَأْيُكَ فِي هَذَا " . فَقَالَ رَجُلٌ مِنْ اَشْرَافِ النَّاسِ، هَذَا وَاللّٰهِ حَرِيٌّ إِنْ خَطَبَ اَنْ يُنْكَحَ، وَاِن شَفَعَ اَن يُشَفَّعَ. قَالَ فَسَكَتَ رَسُولُ اللّٰهِ صلى الله عليه وسلم ثُمَّ مَرَّ رَجُلٌ فَقَالَ لَهُ رَسُولُ اللّٰهِ صلى الله عليه وسلم " مَارَأْيُكَ فِي هَذَا " . فَقَالَ يَا رَسُولَ اللّٰهِ هَذَا رَجُلٌ مِنْ فُقَرَاءِ الْمُسْلِمِينَ، هَذَا حَرِيٌّ اِنْ خَطَبَ اَنْ لاَيُنْكَحَ،وَاِنْ شَفَعَ اَنْ لاَيُشَفَّعَ، وَاِنْ قَال اَنْ لاَ يُسْمَعَ لِقَوْلِهِ. فَقَالَ رَسُولُ اللّٰهِ صلى الله عليه وسلم " هَذَا خَيْرٌ مِنْ مِلْءِ الاَرْضِ مِثْلَ هذا " (البخاري)

Abū 'l-ʿAbbās Sahl ibn Saʿadas-Saʿadī ؓ relates that a person passed by the Holy Prophet ﷺ and the Prophet ﷺ asked one of the Companions that was sitting with him: "what do you think of this man, who has just passed this way?" The companion replied, "He is one of the noblest (or gentlest) of men, and by Allah, if he proposes marriage with any woman, his proposal should be accepted, and if he should recommend, his recommendations should prove effective."[16] *And the Holy Prophet ﷺ kept quiet. Then another man passed by and the Prophet ﷺ asked, "What is your opinion of this man." The companion replied, "He belongs to the class of poor Muslims. If he goes for marriage his proposal will be turned down; if he were to intercede on behalf of any person, his intercession would be rejected; and if he were to speak nobody would listen to him." The Holy Prophet ﷺ said, "If everyone in the world were like the first man, this man would be better than them all."*[17]

The first person described is someone highly respected in the community. The second person described is an indigent of no apparent consequence. But the first is proud and arrogant, and full of all sorts of bad

---

[16]The wording of the ḥadīth states, *in shafaʿa yushafaʿ*. This is often mistranslated as, "If he should recommend someone, his recommendation would be accepted;" however, the correct translation is, "If he should intercede, his intercession would be accepted." This description indicates that person is from the highest elite of society.

[17]Bukhārī, Muslim, Ibn Mājah, Aḥmad.

manners, while the second is humble and sincere. Although both pray, fast, give charity and do hajj, their actions will be weighed in accordance with what is in their hearts. Again, we find the same dichotomy that separated Cain and Abel.

These *aḥādīth* of the Prophet ﷺ, narrated by authentic sources, demonstrate that Islam requires more than just outward adherence to its five pillars. It also requires us to overcome the diseases of the ego and approach those acts of worship with sincerity and purity of heart. If we do not, all that we have done in the way of worship may come to naught and we may face disaster of Judgment Day, for Allah ﷻ said:

وَقَدِمْنَا إِلَى مَا عَمِلُوا مِنْ عَمَلٍ فَجَعَلْنَاهُ هَبَاءً مَّنثُورًا

And We shall turn to whatever deeds they did (in this life), and We shall make such deeds as floating dust scattered about.[18]

SPIRITUALITY: POWER OF THE BELIEVER

Spirituality is the most powerful weapon we can call upon in this struggle between acceptance and non-acceptance, belief or unbelief. When someone's faith becomes weak, it can ultimately reach the point of questioning the very Existence of Allah ﷻ. On the other hand, when *Īmān* increases by means of spiritual support, then the commanding self, *an-Nafs al-Ammāra,* becomes weaker and one begins to see increased success in the struggle against doubt.

However, spirituality, too, must be developed. While many people today like to speak about spirituality in the abstract, few discuss the practical tools of spiritual development. These include:

1) The Sunnah of the Prophet ﷺ: *as-Sunnat an-Nabawīyya.*

2) Knowledge of the Qur'ān: *at-Tarbīyya al-Qurānīyya.*

These are the two doors to spiritual development. They are the instruments of spiritual advancement and the vehicles that lead to the purification of the self, which is the fundamental requirement for achieving

---

[18]Sūratu 'l-Furqān, [The Criterion], 25:22-23.

the full realization of the positive potential with which Allah ﷻ has endowed human beings from birth, according to the *ḥādīth*:

حديث أبي هريرة رضي الله عنه أن النبي صلى الله عليه وسلم قال: "ما من مولود إلا يولد على الفطرة فأبواه يهودانه أو ينصرانه أو يمجسانه كما تنتج البهيمة بهيمة جمعاء هل تحسون فيها من جدعاء"

Abū Hurayrah reported that the Prophet of Allah ﷺ said, "Every child is born upon the natural disposition [of Islam], then it is his parents who make him Jewish, or Christian, or Magian (Zoroastrian), just as an animal delivers a perfect baby animal; do you find it maimed?"[19]

Allah ﷻ speaks of the need for self-purification in the Holy Qur'ān:

قَدْ أَفْلَحَ مَن زَكَّاهَا وَقَدْ خَابَ مَن دَسَّاهَا

Verily, the one who purified it [the self] succeeded and the one who fails corrupts it.[20]

How, then, can we learn to use these two tools? First, we need someone who can analyze these sources and deduce the principles and hidden knowledge within each to extract the methodology of self-purification. One cannot ask kindergarten students to deduce these principles and methods from the Holy Qur'ān and *ḥādīth*. This requires scholars well-versed in these areas of knowledge in order to produce an edible fruit.

Even the most learned scholars of external knowledge may not be able to plumb these depths of this subtle science. Consider the case of Imām al-Ghazālī. Although he was one of the greatest scholars in Shariʿah, he was unable to save himself from the sicknesses of his ego until he followed the way of the seekers, Gnostics and ascetics whose whole lives were focused on training people to overcome such maladies of the self and raise their level of spirituality. Once Imām al-Ghazālī became a student in that school, he began to accumulate extraordinary powers, and spiritual energy until his soul was purified and Divine Light poured into his heart. Since his faith had been built up and established on a firm footing, he was able to leave all that is forbidden, ḥarām. Prior to that, despite his erudition and learning, he had

---

19 Bukhārī and Muslim.
20 Sūratu 'sh-Shams [The Sun], 91:9,10.

always been questioning himself and questioning whatever was around him. He understood the external realities of Islam, but he needed to build up his faith.

He was able to do so by following Qur'ānic prescriptions regarding the heart and its importance, through remembrance of Allah, *dhikrullāh,* and the purification of the self, *Tazkīyyat an-Nafs.* These practices and disciplines allowed him to reach a level of firmness in faith that could not be undermined by doubt; rather, the Station of *Iḥsān* was pulling him up. When Allah ﷻ sees that the seeker has achieved that state where he no longer allows the lower self to pull him down, that seeker is no longer alone: the Lord is with him, observing all that he does. When that belief becomes rooted in the heart, the seeker can no longer fall into major sins.

THE SCHOOL OF *TAZKIYYA*: THE QUR'ANIC SCIENCE OF TREATING THE SELF

The practices that enabled Imām al-Ghazālī to reach this sublime state that is the goal of all seekers can be traced back to the Prophet ﷺ. They are derived from the Holy Qur'ān, as well as from his own practices and those teachings that he shared with his Companions as recorded in the *Sunnah.*

That school of which the Ṣaḥāba partook did not die with the passing of the Prophet ﷺ. Each of the Companions became a school from which the Ummah derived its learning of these methods and knowledge of *Tazkīyyat an-Nafs,* or self-purification. With the passing of time, these schools developed and formalized their methods and created a distinct science termed the Science of *Taṣawwuf.* Just as the schools of Shariʿah was formalized in the first three centuries of Islam, so too did distinct schools of *Taṣawwuf* form to pass on this knowledge to succeeding generations of Muslims. And just as the Shariʿah did not develop outside the framework of Islam, the Qur'ān and the *Sunnah,* even though it branches and knowledge encompassed many areas not mentioned specifically in these sources, so too did *Taṣawwuf* develop based on the framework established by the Qur'ān and the *Sunnah.*

The traditional scholars of Islam understood these realities and attained these states themselves, and they began to set forth the principles, methodologies and disciplines that would allow others to follow in their footsteps so that this science would be preserved for future generations. They did this, because they heeded the warning of the Prophet ﷺ, who said:

ان رسول الله صلى الله عليه وسلم قال خيركم قرني.ثم الذين يلونهم. ثم الذين يلونهم .ثم الذين يلونهم. "

The Prophet ﷺ said, "The best of you is my time then the one that follows it then the one that follows it."[21]

As Islamic civilization and culture devolved, these scholars began to see the rapid reappearance of spiritual maladies, such as love of the self, hypocrisy, showing off, lying, backbiting, hatred, envy, jealousy and countless others. They said began codifying the curricula of the science of self-purification as a means of countering this epidemic. Clearly, then, this science and the disciplines it prescribes are not something innovated, but something that has always been part of Islam and Islamic practice. Moreover, they are the only cure for the disease that has always threatened the heart of humanity since Cain first raised his hand against his brother.

A clear example of the way in which these great scholars responded to the degradation of Muslim morals and manners is that of Imām Shāfiʿī. After establishing his school of thought in Baghdad, he traveled to Cairo where he saw that the people were more corrupt and therefore modified his rulings in order to treat the illnesses he witnessed there. The medications of the heart change over time. Just as modern medical science is constantly creating new treatments for disease, so have the prescriptions of this science evolved over time. In each era, the scholars of *Tazkīyyat an-Nafs* have established different treatments in order to accommodate the prevailing social, political and historical situations.

This is one example from a vast multitude of scholars, beginning immediately after the era of the Prophet ﷺ until today, who sought to establish methods for extricating human beings caught between good and evil. These luminaries established a spiritual curriculum, *ʿal-manhaj ar-rūḥīʿ*, and followed it rigorously. They transformed their faith from something theoretical and abstract into something real and practicable, *Maqām al-Īmān*. In doing so, they made it part of their lives. They believed in Allah ﷻ with

---

[21]Muslim.

genuine conviction, and that conviction was constant and unshakeable. They showed Muslims by their example the importance of self-purification and demonstrated the need for such a disciplined methodology.

Their curricula formed the basis for *tarbīyyat ar-rūḥīyya,* or spiritual training. They developed a school with its own course of study, its own programs, its own methodologies and its own proofs within the context of the Qur'ān and *Sunnah.*

All scholars of this science know that the Qur'ān is the seal of all religious books and the last book sent by Allah ﷻ to humanity. As such, they take it as the primary medical text for treating the ailments of the self.

In the Holy Qur'ān, Allah ﷻ has emphasized the heart, the states of the heart, the situation of the heart, and the struggle against the ego and its desires. From this, these scholars learned the science of treating the heart and its maladies. They learned this science by studying the many verses in the Holy Qur'ān that discuss the purification of the self, that analyze the ego and its desires, that talk about love and fear. They also studied the many verses that describe the heart and the soul, that define love, humbleness and repentance. Their understandings were expanded by their study of those verses that focus on piety, certainty, familiarity, nearness and happiness, as well as those that discuss hypocrisy, liars, heretics and conspiracies and provide clear instruction on the avoidance of these. They also found verses on how to remember Allah ﷻ in a hidden way or in a hidden place, verses on the benefits of waking up at night to perform *Qīyām al-Layl* and the *tahajjud* prayer. They found many verses describing the state of *Iḥsān* and detailing the steps necessary to reach it.

These scholars found further examples in the *Sunnah* of the Prophet ﷺ. They studied how he taught his Companions to rid themselves of these same diseases, as exemplified by his famous statement:

قدمتم خير مقدم وقدمتم من الجهاد الأصغر الى الجهاد الأكبر مجاهدة العبد هواه.

On the authority of Jābir:

The Prophet came back from one of his campaigns saying: "You have come forth in the best way of coming forth: you have come from the smaller jihad to the greater jihad." They said: "And what is the greater jihad?" He replied: "The striving (mujāhadat) of Allah's servants against their idle desires."[22]

The scholar Ibn Qayyim defined fourteen forms of jihad. Only one of these involves war or combat; the other thirteen represent various manifestations of struggle of a person with himself, society, education and development. To struggle against the self—to control and command it—is essential to harvesting the fruits of spirituality. It is required of one who would purify himself and become truly conscious of Allah ﷻ and fearful of His Displeasure. To do this, the seeker wages jihad against his bad desires and makes Allah ﷻ, His Prophet ﷺ and the excellent morals and manners they enjoined his goal.

THE IMPORTANCE OF REMEMBRANCE

The means that such "fighters in the Way of Allah" use to accomplish this purification is *dhikrullāh*, the Remembrance of Allah, for Allah ﷻ said:

وَاذْكُر رَّبَّكَ فِي نَفْسِكَ تَضَرُّعاً وَخِيفَةً وَدُونَ الْجَهْرِ مِنَ الْقَوْلِ بِالْغُدُوِّ وَالآصَالِ
وَلاَ تَكُن مِّنَ الْغَافِلِينَ

And do (O Muhammad) remember your Lord within yourself humbly and with awe, in a hidden manner, at morn and evening. And be not of the neglectful.[23].

To "remember your Lord in a hidden manner" indicates an inner recitation and remembrance. That is why the Holy Qur'ān is filled with verses regarding *dhikrullāh.*

The Holy Qur'ān and the *Sunnah* of the Prophet ﷺ represent the constitution of the Muslims. Every aspect of our existence is covered therein: morality, jurisprudence, politics, economics, social behavior and of course religion. They also cover the most important subject of all, which is the knowledge of self-purification.

---

[22]Al-Khaṭṭābī in his *Ṭārīkh*, Īmām Ghazālī in his *Iḥyā'* and al-ʿIrāqī said that Bayhaqī related it on the authority of Jābir.
[23]Sūratu 'l-ʿArāf [The Heights], 7:205.

While this science is essential to practicing the essence of the religion, it is far more subtle than the outward forms and is thus often ignored or overlooked. Today, we see many people studying questions of Islam and economics, we see Muslims debating *Fiqh* and reciting poetry, but almost no one is interested in learning how to purify the self. Yet, *Tazkīyyat an-Nafs* is what the Prophet ﷺ spent his life engaged in. And when asked by his wife ʿĀ'ishā ؓ, why he was so preoccupied in devotions, to the point his legs were swollen, his answer was, "And should I not be a thankful servant?"

This, then, is the science of *taṣawwuf,* from which the term "Sufism" is derived.

CRITICISMS OF SUFISM

Today, the word "Sufism" is problematic for some people because of some so-called Sufis who delved deeply into philosophy and theology and came up with things that were not accepted or not understood. This debate is beyond the scope of our discussion. Suffice it to say that Allah ﷻ mentioned *ʿIlm Tazkīyyat an-Nafs* in the Holy Qur'ān, and whatever Allah ﷻ said must be obeyed. The Sufi scholars, including Imām al-Ghazālī and many other luminaries such as Junayd al-Baghdādī, Sulaymān ad-Dārānī, Sirr as-Saqatī, ʿAbd al-Qādir Jilānī and countless others, all imposed the condition on their students that they follow Allah's Holy Book and the Prophetic *Sunnah.* It is worth noting that even Ibn Taymīyya, one of the strictest scholars, accepted authentic *taṣawwuf* and even went so far as to define the three different levels of *taṣawwuf* in his renowned *Fatawā.*

Another criticism leveled at the Sufis is that they renounce the world. Often those who look at Sufism from outside imagine the Sufis to be philosophers and theologians who have turned their backs on everything to sit in their own retreats. However, the science of *taṣawwuf* in the main, while calling for asceticism, does not call for permanent withdrawal from the world. Rather, it uses the methodology of seclusion for periods of time, to help the seeker purge love of *dunyā*—his love of wealth, fame and status—from his heart. Such asceticism of the heart enables a sincere Muslim to override *dunyā* and put it under his control, moving in whatever way he likes for sake of Allah ﷻ. Such a person, if he is of good means, may use whatever he has of *dunyā* wealth in the way of Allah ﷻ, rather than using it purely for self-gratification. Such a person will spend freely in the Way of

Allah ﷻ, for it has no meaning to him: "He owns the *dunyā* while the *dunyā* does not own him."

THE DIFFERENT SCHOOLS OF SPIRITUALITY

The Prophet ﷺ said:

اختلاف أمتي رحمة للناس

The differences between my nation is a mercy.[24]

We see this, too, in the schools of spirituality. The methods may change from one teacher to another, but the goal remains the same. That goal is self-purification and spiritual advancement.

Allah ﷻ said in the Holy Qur'ān:

وَالَّذِينَ جَاهَدُوا فِينَا لَنَهْدِيَنَّهُمْ سُبُلَنَا وَإِنَّ اللهَ لَمَعَ الْمُحْسِنِينَ

But as for those who strive hard in Our cause, We shall most certainly guide them onto ways that lead unto Us, for behold, Allah is indeed with the doers of good.[25]

This verse mentions not one, but multiple ways for the seeker to reach his Lord. Due to this multiplicity of paths, this science developed countless methodologies, each one different than the other, and yet all constrained by Allah's Divine Law, Shariʿah. However, all these branches stem from a common trunk, a single foundation, and that is *dhikrullāh*. The goal of each is Allah ﷻ: to declare His Oneness and His Uniqueness and to make His remembrance.

Collectively, these paths became a means for transporting Muslims on their spiritual journey, raising believers higher and higher until they reached the state of Iḥsān. It is a science firmly grounded in the ḥādīth and the Holy Qur'ān, the science of self-purification or *ʿIlm Tazkīyyat an-Nafs*.

---

[24]Al-Ḥāfiẓ al-ʿIrāqī, al-Ḥāfiẓ as-Sakhāwī, *Maqāsid al-ḥasana* p. 49, #39 from Ibn al-Ḥājib in the *Mukhtaṣar*. Al-Khaṭṭābī mentions it in the context of a digression in *Gharīb al-ḥadīth*.
[25]Sūratu 'l-ʿAnkabūt [The Spider], 29:69.

THE STRUGGLE AGAINST THE SELF

The fruit of *Tazkīyyat an-Nafs* is to reach the Station of Perfect Character, *Iḥsān*, as the Prophet ﷺ mentioned when asked by Sayyidina Jibrīl ؑ.

As we have already explained, *Iḥsān* is the highest level of *Īmān* that the seeker can develop through his quest for reality. This is what we call *al-Yaqīn al-Ḥaqīqī*; the Reality of Certainty and knowing that brings true understanding and leads to *al-Īmānash-Shuhūdī*, the true faith of witnessing the signs of Allah's Oneness everywhere. The only higher level of realization is *Maqām al-Iḥsān*. At this Station of Perfection, the seeker realizes that Allah ﷻ is observing him in every moment. Through this realization, he is able to perfect his behavior. Then the seeker attains the genuine realization that he is observing Allah ﷻ. That is why meditation becomes a necessity, for it is through this practice that the seeker is able to reach this high level.

That is why Allah ﷻ specifically mentioned meditation, *tafakkur*, in the Holy Qur'ān:

الَّذِينَ يَذْكُرُونَ اللَّهَ قِيَامًا وَقُعُودًا وَعَلَىٰ جُنُوبِهِمْ وَيَتَفَكَّرُونَ فِي خَلْقِ السَّمَاوَاتِ وَالْأَرْضِ رَبَّنَا مَا
خَلَقْتَ هَٰذَا بَاطِلًا سُبْحَانَكَ فَقِنَا عَذَابَ النَّارِ

Men who celebrate the praises of Allah, standing, sitting, and lying down on their sides, and contemplate the (wonders of) creation in the Heavens and the Earth, (With the thought): "Our Lord! not for nothing Have You created (all) this! Glory to You! Give us salvation from the penalty of the Fire."[26]

This verse speaks of those who are focusing on their Lord intently. At the same time, Allah ﷻ is looking at them and with His Gaze, He is propelling them upward. It is of this level of spiritual attainment that the Qur'ān speaks when it says:

وَسَخَّرَ لَكُم مَّا فِي السَّمَاوَاتِ وَمَا فِي الْأَرْضِ جَمِيعًا مِّنْهُ إِنَّ فِي ذَٰلِكَ لَآيَاتٍ لِّقَوْمٍ يَتَفَكَّرُونَ

Whatever is in the Heavens and in the Earth will be made subject to you.[27]

---

[26]Sūrat Āli-'Imrān [The Family of 'Imrān], 3:191.
[27]Sūratu 'l-Jāthīya [The Crouching], 45:13.

Here, "Heavens" refers to the realm of the spirit, while "Earth" refers to the realm of the body. That power enables the seeker to leave all that Allah ﷻ has forbidden us on the physical plane and to practice all that we have been ordered in the way of physical, earthly obligations. It enables the seeker to perfect his spiritual manners. All this is achieved within the framework of *Sharīʿatullāh.* In this way, the spirit is connected to the real meaning of the verses of the Holy Qur'ān and the *Sunnah* of the Prophet ﷺ.

Consider the example of Ḥāritha, when he was asked by the Prophet ﷺ in what state he awoke:

عَنْ أَنَسِ بْنِ مَالِكٍ ، قَالَ : بَيْنَمَا رَسُولُ اللهِ صَلَّى اللهُ عَلَيْهِ وَسَلَّمَ يَمْشِي إِذِ اسْتَقْبَلَهُ شَابٌّ مِنَ الأَنْصَارِ ، فَقَالَ لَهُ النَّبِيُّ صَلَّى اللهُ عَلَيْهِ وَسَلَّمَ : " كَيْفَ أَصْبَحْتَ يَا حَارِثُ ؟ " قَالَ : أَصْبَحْتُ مُؤْمِنًا بِاللهِ عَزَّ وَجَلَّ حَقًّا . قَالَ : " انْظُرْ مَا تَقُولُ ، فَإِنَّ لِكُلِّ قَوْلٍ حَقِيقَةً " . قَالَ : يَا رَسُولَ اللهِ عَزَفَتْ نَفْسِي عَنِ الدُّنْيَا ، فَأَسْهَرْتُ لَيْلِي ، وَأَظْمَأْتُ نَهَارِي ، وَكَأَنِّي بِعَرْشِ رَبِّي عَزَّ وَجَلَّ بَارِزًا ، وَكَأَنِّي أَنْظُرُ إِلَى أَهْلِ الْجَنَّةِ يَتَزَاوَرُونَ فِيهَا ، وَكَأَنِّي أَنْظُرُ إِلَى أَهْلِ النَّارِ يَتَعَاوَوْنَ فِيهَا ، قَالَ : " أَبْصَرْتَ ، فَالْزَمْ عَبْدًا نَوَّرَ اللهُ الإِيمَانَ فِي قَلْبِهِ "

> *Anas ibn Mālik reported that the Prophet ﷺ asked Ḥāritha ibn an-Nuʿmān ؓ, "How did you find yourself this morning?" And he replied, "I found myself this morning a believer in Allah in truth." The Prophet ﷺ said, "Every statement has its verification. So, what is the verification of your faith?" Ḥāritha replied, "My soul has become averse to the dunyā and fled from it. So, I have made my night sleepless [i.e. through tahajjud and night-time ʿibādah] and made my day full of thirst [i.e. through constant fasting] and it is now as if I am right in front of the Throne (ʿArsh) of my Lord. And it is as if I am gazing upon the people of Paradise visiting each other [in joy] and as if I am gazing upon the people of the Fire trying to help each other in the Fire." The Prophet ﷺ replied, "You have gained true vision; so hold fast to it (abṣarta, f'alzam)." [Speaking to Anas, he then said:] "[He is] a servant whose heart Allah has enlightened with faith."*[28]

---

[28]Al-ʿAskarī in his *Amthāl,* and aṭ-Ṭabarānī in his *Kabīr,* an-Najjār and al-Bazzār with variant wordings: *ʿArāfta fa 'lzam,* "You realized, so continue on what you are doing," *Kanzu 'l-ʿummāl.* #36990.

When Ḥāritha said, "I made my night sleepless and my days thirsty," it means he opposed his ego by waking up at night for prayer and working very hard during the day while fasting. When Ḥāritha said, "I woke up as if I am looking at the Throne," note that he did not relate it as if he saw it in a dream; rather, he said, "As if I am looking up high at the Throne of Allah and as if I am looking at the people of Paradise," and, "as if I am looking at the people of the Fire," for Ḥāritha had reached the highest level of *Īmān ash-shuhūdī*, and the Prophet ﷺ asked for proof of his claim, "For every saying there is a proof." Ḥāritha's proof was to perceive with his eyes the realities of the Afterlife. Out of good manners, he said, "as if," in order not to show off his state before the Master of Masters, Sayyidina Muhammad ﷺ, although he had, in fact, achieved *yaqīn*, full certainty of what he had witnessed.

THE HEART AS KEY TO SPIRITUAL IMPROVEMENT

The Holy Qur'ān contains at least 130 verses that mention the heart (either as *qalb* and *fūād*). Let us look within the Holy Qur'ān to see what Allah ﷻ has mentioned to us on the importance of this organ:

أَلَمْ يَأْنِ لِلَّذِينَ آمَنُوا أَن تَخْشَعَ قُلُوبُهُمْ لِذِكْرِ اللَّهِ وَمَا نَزَلَ مِنَ الْحَقِّ وَلَا يَكُونُوا كَالَّذِينَ أُوتُوا الْكِتَابَ مِن
قَبْلُ فَطَالَ عَلَيْهِمُ الْأَمَدُ فَقَسَتْ قُلُوبُهُمْ وَكَثِيرٌ مِّنْهُمْ فَاسِقُونَ

Is not the time ripe for the hearts of those who believe to submit to Allah's reminder and to the truth that is revealed, that they become not as those who received the Scripture of old but the term was prolonged for them and so their hearts were hardened, and many of them are evil-livers. [29]

وَلَيْسَ عَلَيْكُمْ جُنَاحٌ فِيمَا أَخْطَأْتُم بِهِ وَلَٰكِن مَّا تَعَمَّدَتْ قُلُوبُكُمْ وَكَانَ اللَّهُ غَفُورًا رَّحِيمًا

And there is no sin for you in the mistakes that you make unintentionally, but what your hearts purpose (that will be a sin for you). Allah is Forgiving, Merciful.[30]

لَّا يُؤَاخِذُكُمُ اللَّهُ بِاللَّغْوِ فِي أَيْمَانِكُمْ وَلَٰكِن يُؤَاخِذُكُم بِمَا كَسَبَتْ قُلُوبُكُمْ وَاللَّهُ غَفُورٌ حَلِيمٌ

[29]Sūratu 'l-Ḥadīd [Iron], 57:16.
[30]Sūratu 'l-Aḥzāb [The Confederates], 33:5.

Allah will not call you to account for thoughtlessness in your oaths [laghaw fī aymanikkum], but for the intention in your hearts, and He is Oft-Forgiving, Most Forbearing.[31]

All of the verses that mention the heart contain clues to understanding and treating its diseases, and these are elaborated upon by the teachings of the Prophet ﷺ:

الا وان في الجسد مضغة اذاصلحت صلح الجسد كله، واذا فسدت فسد الجسد كله الا وهي القلب.

The Prophet ﷺ said, "In the body there is a small piece of flesh; if that piece of flesh is rectified then the whole body will be rectified and if it becomes corrupt then the whole body will become corrupt, and truly that is the heart."[32]

The Prophet ﷺ emphasized the importance of the heart in this, and many other *ḥādīths*. The Holy Qur'ān's mention of the heart and its condition is so emphatic and frequent that it ties everything human beings do to the condition and state of the heart.

The heart that is enlightened is the one that will move the mind and the senses towards what is virtuous and away from all that is corrupt. Unfortunately, that is not the condition of most hearts.

DISEASES OF THE HEART

The Qur'ān describes the diseased heart as *marīd al-qalb,* signifying hypocrisy, doubt, suspicion, deviance, heedlessness and oppression. We shall deal with each of these conditions separately.

---

[31]Sūratu 'l-Baqarah [The Heifer], 2:225. *Laghaw* is to swear to something loosely, such as, "I swear I did not do that." It is not a genuine oath, but rather a habit of the tongue to use Allah's Name in affirmation or negation. The Prophet ﷺ excused the Ṣaḥāba for such things. Allah ﷻ will not accept such oaths if one swears in His Name by tongue but rejects it in one's heart; rather, this incurs His punishment.

[32]Bukhārī and Muslim.

THE HYPOCRITICAL HEART

The most dangerous illness of the heart is hypocrisy. That is why Allah ﷻ described the *munāfiqūn*, hypocrites, as those who:

يَقُولُونَ بِأَلْسِنَتِهِم مَّا لَيْسَ فِي قُلُوبِهِمْ

(They) say with their tongues what is not in their hearts.[33]

This means that they conspire in their hearts, while outwardly appearing good. Such was the behavior of the hypocrites of al-Madīna with the Prophet ﷺ and his Companions. Such people are extremely dangerous, which is why Allah ﷻ warned about them many times in the Qur'ān. They were those who demonstrated their obedience to the Prophet ﷺ with one hand while stabbing him in the back with the other.

However, this disease was not limited to that time and place. There are many Muslims who stab their brothers and sisters in the back while appearing friendly to their faces. Moreover, hypocrisy leads to other serious illnesses, such lying, killing, harming, and cheating. Allah ﷻ said to those who have this illness:

أَفَلَا يَتَدَبَّرُونَ الْقُرْآنَ أَمْ عَلَى قُلُوبٍ أَقْفَالُهَا

Will they then not meditate on the Qur'ān, or are there locks on the hearts?[34]

The key to that lock is found in the Holy Qur'ān. However, when the heart is drowned in the ocean of sin, that key to salvation is lost. The lock of hypocrisy bars the way to the path of guidance. This is a dangerous state from which the sinner may never return to the path of truth, for the Qur'ān says:

كَذَلِكَ يَطْبَعُ اللَّهُ عَلَى قُلُوبِ الَّذِينَ لَا يَعْلَمُونَ

Thus does Allah seal the hearts of those who know not.[35]

---

[33] Sūratu 'l-Fatḥ [Victory], 48:11.
[34] Sūrah Muḥammad, 47:24.
[35] Sūrah Rūm [Rome], 30:59.

The meaning of this verse is that Allah ﷻ will leave those who make no effort to return to right guidance to their own devices. It is for this reason that He also said:

إِنَّكَ لَا تَهْدِي مَنْ أَحْبَبْتَ وَلَكِنَّ اللهَ يَهْدِي مَن يَشَاء وَهُوَ أَعْلَمُ بِالْمُهْتَدِينَ

It is true you (O Muhammad) will not be able to guide every one whom you love; but Allah guides those whom He will and He knows best those who receive guidance.[36]

THE DOUBTING HEART

Allah ﷻ said:

إِنَّمَا يَسْتَأْذِنُكَ الَّذِينَ لَا يُؤْمِنُونَ بِاللهِ وَالْيَوْمِ الآخِرِ وَارْتَابَتْ قُلُوبُهُمْ فَهُمْ فِي رَيْبِهِمْ يَتَرَدَّدُونَ

Only those will request exemption from you (O Muhammad) those who do not believe in Allah and the Last Day, and whose hearts are in doubt, so that they are tossed in their doubts to and fro.[37]

Those described here have an illness that causes doubts to emerge in their hearts and when they try to strive sincerely in Allah's Way they cannot because of the faltering of their hearts. That is the first disease of the heart: doubts which cause hesitation.

THE SUSPICIOUS HEART

Suspicion about the intents and motives of others is a lesser disease that causes the sufferer to imagine that other people are out to get them.

About this, Allah ﷻ said:

يَا أَيُّهَا الَّذِينَ آمَنُوا اجْتَنِبُوا كَثِيرًا مِّنَ الظَّنِّ إِنَّ بَعْضَ الظَّنِّ إِثْمٌ

O you who believe! Avoid suspicion as much (as possible) for suspicion in some cases is a sin.[38]

---

[36]Sūratu 'l-Qaṣaṣ [The Stories], 28:56.
[37]Sūratu 't-Tawbah [Repentance], 9:45.
[38]Sūratu 'l-Ḥujurāt [The Private Apartments], 49:12.

This means avoid harboring bad thoughts about others, for most of such suspicion is fallacious and will lead to error.

THE DEVIATED HEART

Those whose hearts are deviated become rude and constricted. Of them, Allah ﷻ said:

فَأَمَّا الَّذِينَ فِي قُلُوبِهِمْ زَيْغٌ فَيَتَّبِعُونَ مَا تَشَابَهَ مِنْهُ ابْتِغَاء الْفِتْنَةِ وَابْتِغَاء تَأْوِيلِهِ

But those in whose hearts is perversity follow the part thereof that is allegorical, seeking discord and searching for its hidden meanings, but no one knows its hidden meanings except Allah.[39]

THE HEEDLESS HEART

The heedless heart is one that is asleep and unable to see. This is one of greatest problems Muslims face. There can be no true belief without the ability perceive reality and truth.

About those afflicted with this ailment, Allah ﷻ said:

وَلَا تَعْدُ عَيْنَاكَ عَنْهُمْ تُرِيدُ زِينَةَ الْحَيَاةِ الدُّنْيَا وَلَا تُطِعْ مَنْ أَغْفَلْنَا قَلْبَهُ عَن ذِكْرِنَا وَاتَّبَعَ هَوَاهُ وَكَانَ أَمْرُهُ فُرُطًا

Nor obey any whose heart We have permitted to neglect the remembrance of Us, one who follows his own desires, whose case has gone beyond all bounds.[40]

Such a heart is directed by *lahwa al-qalb,* bad desires, an illness from which most Muslims suffer, as Allah ﷻ said:

لَاهِيَةً قُلُوبُهُمْ وَأَسَرُّواْ النَّجْوَى

Their hearts set on passing delights, yet they who are [thus] bent on wrongdoing conceal their innermost thoughts.[41]

---

[39] Sūrat Āli-'Imrān [The Family of 'Imrān], 3:7.
[40] Sūratu 'l-Kahf [The Cave], 18:28.
[41] Sūratu 'l-Anbīyā [The Prophets], 21:3.

THE OPPRESSIVE HEART

وعنه أن رسول الله صلى الله عليه وسلم قال أتدرون ما المفلس؟ قالوا المفلس فينا من لا درهم له ولا متاع . فقال إن المفلس من أمتي من يأتي يوم القيامة بصلاة وصيام وزكاة ويأتي وقد شتم هذا وقذف هذا . وأكل مال هذا . وسفك دم هذا وضرب هذا فيعطى هذا من حسناته وهذا من حسناته فإن فنيت حسناته قبل أن يقضى ما عليه أخذ من خطاياهم فطرحت عليه ثم طرح في النار . رواه مسلم

Sayyidina Abū Hurayrah related that the Prophet once asked his companions, "Do you know who is considered bankrupt?" The companions replied, "The bankrupt one is he who owns neither dirham nor property." The Prophet said, "The bankrupt one from among my followers is he who will come on the Day of Judgment with a good record of ṣalāt, ṣawm and zakāt, and yet he had abused someone and slandered another. He had usurped the goods of another person, he killed someone and beat yet another person. So then one person [whom he afflicted] will come and he will give him from his good deeds and another will come and take from them and if his good deeds are finished before he can fulfill what is due to them then their wrong deeds will be taken from them and thrown on him and then he will in the end be thrown in the Fire."

One would think it impossible that someone with a good record of *ṣalāt*, *ṣawm* and *zakāt* be spiritually bankrupt because most Muslims would describe Islam as the five pillars, believing that anyone who performs them is safe. Yet, here the Prophet ﷺ describes someone who did all these in just such a lamentable position.

This demonstrates that there is no benefit of the prayer and fasting for someone who conspired against his brother, spread harmful rumors, cheated, stole, lied or abused others. All these corrupt traits must be eliminated before those acts of worship can benefit one.

Consider another example from the *ḥādīth*:

يا خولة! رب متخوض في مال الله ومال رسوله فيما اشتهت نفسه له النار يوم القيامة.

Khawla bint ʿAmir –, the wife of Sayyidina Ḥamza ؓ related that the Prophet ﷺ said to her, "O Khawla! Perhaps someone may misappropriate Allah's

Properties and His Prophet's properties in whatever their selves desire; for him is the Fire on Judgment Day."[42]

Today one sees how much money and wealth Muslims misappropriate from what belongs to Allah ﷻ and His Prophet ﷺ, all the while observing all Five Pillars of Islam fastidiously. Often those in charge of collecting the *zakāt*, though they pray and fast, misuse the *Bayt al-Māl* and other charities designated for the poor and orphans. Because of their wrongdoing, all of their worship will be thrown in their faces and such people are destined for the fire on Judgment Day. These are examples of the ways in which the sickness of oppression leads people into sin, despite their adherence to the outward requirements of Islam.

The Prophet ﷺ said:

أخوف ما أخاف على أمتي من عالم فصيح اللسان جهول القلب

The thing I fear most for my community is a scholar with an eloquent tongue but whose heart is ignorant.

He ﷺ also said:

أخْوفُ ما أخاف على أمتي كل منافق عليم اللسان.

The thing I fear most for my community is a hypocrite eloquent of tongue but whose heart is ignorant.[43]

The Prophet ﷺ feared that people would follow religious scholars who were well-versed in the teachings of religion and adept at presenting them, but whose hearts did not reflect the status and realities of what they teach, as Allah ﷻ said:

يَا أَيُّهَا الَّذِينَ آمَنُوا لِمَ تَقُولُونَ مَا لَا تَفْعَلُونَ كَبُرَ مَقْتًا عِندَ اللهِ أَن تَقُولُوا مَا لَا تَفْعَلُونَ

O you who believe! Why say you that which you do not know? Grievously odious is it in the sight of Allah that you say that which you do not know![44]

---

[42]Aṭ-Ṭabarānī in his *Kabīr*.

[43]Tirmidhī. Another version is "the thing I fear most for my community is every hypocrite eloquent of tongue."

[44]Sūratu 'ṣ-Ṣaff [The Ranks], 61:2

Doctors and engineers cannot deduce principles of *Fiqh* or *Shari'ah,* nor can they teach the fundamentals and principles of Islam. This position is only for scholars, and scholars who are *al-'ulamāu 'l-'amilīn,* those who practice what they know. Such scholars are pious and sincere men and women, working purely for Allah's sake, not for the sake of a position or a salary. Allah said:

وَلَقَدْ ذَرَأْنَا لِجَهَنَّمَ كَثِيرًا مِّنَ الْجِنِّ وَالإِنسِ لَهُمْ قُلُوبٌ لاَّ يَفْقَهُونَ بِهَا

Many are the Jinns and men we have made for Hell: They have hearts wherewith they understand not... Sūratu 'l-A'rāf [The Heights], 7:179

THE SEVENTEEN RUINOUS TRAITS

These ailments of the heart spawn other bad qualities in the individual. Imām Muhammad al-Busayrī asked Shaykh Abū 'l-Ḥasan al-Kharqānī about the major ruinous traits in human character, and the latter replied that they number seventeen. Each of these traits resembles a great tree, for each has a trunk that is deeply rooted, as well as primary limbs, smaller off-shooting branches, leaves and so on. Each tree is laden with an array of bad manners. The seventeen negative characteristics are listed here in order their impact on the overall human character.

They are known as *al-Akhlāqu 'dh-Dhamīmah,* "the Ruinous Traits" and "the Tree of Bad Manners", which are:

1. Anger (*al-Ghaḍab*)
2. Love of This World (*Ḥubb ad-Dunyā*)
3. Malice (*al-Ḥiqd*)
4. Jealousy (*al-Ḥasad*)
5. Vanity (*al-'Ujb*)
6. Stinginess (*al-Bukhl*)
7. Avarice (*al-Ṭama'*)
8. Cowardice (*al-Jubn*)
9. Indolence (*al-Baṭalah*)
10. Arrogance (*al-Kibr*)
11. Ostentation (*al-Riyā'*)
12. Attachment (*al-Ḥirs*)
13. Superiority (*al-'Aẓamah*)
14. Heedlessness and Laziness (*al-Ghabāwah wa 'l-Kasālah*)
15. Anxiety (*al-Ḥamm*)

16. Depression (*al-Ghamm*)
17. The 800 Forbidden Acts (*al-Manhīyāt*)

Anger is the worst of all seventeen of the ruinous traits. It may easily be said that anger is the source from which the others flow. That is why Allah ﷻ said:

وَالْكَاظِمِينَ الْغَيْظَ وَالْعَافِينَ عَنِ النَّاسِ وَاللهُ يُحِبُّ الْمُحْسِنِينَ

Those who control their wrath and are forgiving toward Mankind; Allah loves the good.[45]

We must purify ourselves from these bad traits and rid our hearts of the underlying ailments that are their source. Outward adherence to the Five Pillars is not enough; we must perfect our behavior.

This requires a program of self-evaluation, purification, seclusion and establishing a practice of remembrance and contemplation under the guidance of an authorized Shaykh of Spiritual Discipline (*Shaykh at-Tarbīyyah).* In this way, the seeker is able to achieve a state in which our heart is able to receive Divine Inspiration and observe Divine Realities.

THE PURIFIED HEART

Just as the diseased heart has its ailments, the purified heart has its own qualities that manifest themselves in the life of the seeker. These include guidance, compassion and enlightenment.

THE GUIDED HEART

At that time the heart is purified, Allah ﷻ makes it a site of revelation and a receiver for the message of truth.

إذا أراد الله تعالى بعبد خيرا جعل له واعظا من نفسه يأمره وينهاه.

The Prophet ﷺ said, "When Allah wants good for His servant, He will give him an advisor in his heart, urging him to good and prohibiting him from wrongdoing."[46]

---

[45]Sūrat Āli 'Imrān [The Family of 'Imrān], 3:134.
[46]ad-Daylamī in *al-Musnad al-Firdaws*, 30762 from Umm Salamah.

The Holy Qur'ān states:

مَّا جَعَلَ اللَّهُ لِرَجُلٍ مِّن قَلْبَيْنِ فِي جَوْفِهِ

Allah did not give two hearts to anyone.[47]

The meaning of this verse is that we cannot divide our heart between Allah ﷻ and this world. The heart is one, and it must be with Allah ﷻ. That why we must eradicate the ruinous traits that begin to fill our heart as we grow from infant to child, child to youth and youth to adult. We must eliminate these characteristics and open our heart so that it becomes a spring from which every individual can come and quench their thirst for knowledge.

من اخلص لله اربعين يوما ظهرت ينابيع الحكمة من قلبه على لسانه

It is related from the Prophet, "Whoever devotes himself sincerely to Allah for forty days, springs of wisdom will emerge from his heart upon his tongue."[48]

THE COMPASSIONATE HEART

Allah ﷻ created human beings with social hearts. He said in the Qur'ān:

ثُمَّ قَفَّيْنَا عَلَى آثَارِهِم بِرُسُلِنَا وَقَفَّيْنَا بِعِيسَى ابْنِ مَرْيَمَ وَآتَيْنَاهُ الْإِنجِيلَ وَجَعَلْنَا فِي قُلُوبِ الَّذِينَ اتَّبَعُوهُ رَأْفَةً وَرَحْمَةً

Then We caused Our messengers to follow in their footsteps; and We caused Jesus, son of Mary, to follow, and gave him the Gospel, and placed compassion and mercy in the hearts of those who followed him.[49]

Thus, He put into the hearts of the believers love and mercy. That is why the Companions used to take care of their community, and even other communities, for their hearts were full of love for Allah ﷻ.

THE ENLIGHTENED HEART

A *ḥādīth* states:

---

[47]Sūratu 'l-Aḥzāb [The Confederates], 33:4.
[48]Abū Na'īm.
[49]Sūratu 'l-Ḥadīd [Iron], 57:27.

ما وسعتني أرضي ولا سمائي ولكن وسعني قلب عبدي المؤمن:يقول الله

My Earth and My Heaven encompass Me not, but the heart of My believing servant encompasses Me.[50]

The heart of a believer can contain his Lord if it is cleansed by self-purification and is longing to contact the Divine Presence. One with such a heart is constantly yearning to obey Allah ﷻ, to serve Him and follow the *Sunnah* of our beloved Prophet ﷺ. Such a one longs to perform acts of supererogatory worship with as much intensity as one whose heart is given over to *dunyā* longs for the pleasures of this world.

The heart has different levels and states. It is even said by the masters of the sciences of self-purification that the heart will go through ascensions that raise it higher and higher.

ان من امتي لرجالا الايمان اثبت في قلوبهم من الجبال الرواسي.

The Prophet said: Verily from my Community are men, in whose hearts the faith is like huge mountains.[51]

PRINCIPLES OF THE SCHOOL OF SPIRITUAL EDUCATION

These excellent qualities cannot be developed without a dedicated effort on the part of the seeker. They come only as the fruits of rigorous spiritual practices as outlined in the traditional curricula or the established schools of *ʿIlm Tazkīyyat an-Nafs.* Such practices cannot be learned from books; rather, they must be learned from one who has already made this journey, an authentic master of spiritual sciences who understands the maladies of the heart and knows how to cure them, a teacher in *al-madrasat ar-rūḥīyy,* the school of spiritual education.

Such schools teach the seeker how to eliminate the illnesses of the heart and the bad characteristics of the ego, and how to build in their stead good characteristics and the excellent qualities of the pure-hearted.

---

[50]Ghazālī, *Iḥyā'*. There are disputes over the authenticity or source of this tradition and some say it is an Isrā'īlī tradition, but there is an overwhelming truth to it according to the tradition narrated by aṭ-Ṭabarānī: "The receptacles of your Lord are the hearts of His righteous servants, the most cherished, gentle and refined to Him."

[51]Ibn Jarīr. *Kanzu 'l-ʿummāl,* 4573.

No doctor ever began to practice without first interning and learning from more experienced physicians in an actual medical ward. No lawyer practiced law without interning with an experienced attorney, assisting with cases and trials in order to learn that which could never be taught in the classroom or written in books. And just as there are schools of diplomacy that teach diplomats how to behave and act, there are schools that teach believers how to act in accordance with Allah's Way and how behave with their Lord, His Prophet ﷺ and with each other.

LOVE OF ALLAH AND FEAR OF ALLAH

The first principles of spiritual education are love of Allah ﷻ and fear of Allah ﷻ. These two principles must be kept foremost in the seeker's mind and heart, for they are the keys to overcoming evil and establishing good. Allah ﷻ said:

قُلْ إِن كُنتُمْ تُحِبُّونَ اللهَ فَاتَّبِعُونِي يُحْبِبْكُمُ اللهُ وَيَغْفِرْ لَكُمْ ذُنُوبَكُمْ وَاللهُ غَفُورٌ رَّحِيمٌ

Say: "If you do love Allah, Follow me: Allah will love you and forgive you your sins: For Allah is Oft-Forgiving, Most Merciful.[52]

To love is to obey. And Allah ﷻ said:

وَأَمَّا مَنْ خَافَ مَقَامَ رَبِّهِ وَنَهَى النَّفْسَ عَنِ الْهَوَى فَإِنَّ الْجَنَّةَ هِيَ الْمَأْوَى

And for such as had entertained the fear of standing before their Lord's (tribunal) and had restrained (their) soul from lower desires. Their abode will be the Garden.[53]

وَلِمَنْ خَافَ مَقَامَ رَبِّهِ جَنَّتَانِ

But for such as fear the time when they will stand before (the Judgment Seat of) their Lord, there will be two Gardens.[54]

Fear of Allah ﷻ will prohibit the self from obeying bad desires. Thus, love of Allah ﷻ and fear of Allah ﷻ are the two bases that will develop the

---

[52]Sūrat Āli-ʿImrān [The Family of ʿImrān], 3:31.
[53]Sūratu 'n-Naziʿat [Those who drag forth], 79:40.
[54]Sūratu 'r-Raḥmān [The Most Merciful], 55:46.

means of approach to Allah ﷻ and His Prophet ﷺ, for indeed those who love and fear Allah ﷻ must also love His Prophet ﷺ, which yields obedience.

EMPTINESS AND SWEETNESS

Another principle is *taknīyya bʿada takhlīyyah,* emptiness followed by sweetness. Purification of the self cannot be accomplished except through *takhlīyyah,* emptying oneself of bad manners. Doing so allows the Divine Sweetness to enter the heart.

Consider the example of Sayyidina Bilāl, one of the Companions of the Prophet. When he was being tortured by Umayyah ibn Khalaf, he repeatedly exclaimed, *"Aḥad, Aḥad"*[55] because he had reached the Station of Vision where he could witness not just the Oneness of Allah ﷻ, but His Absolute Unique Oneness,[56] which is beyond any description. Sayyidina Bilāl had advanced beyond the Station of Witnessing Oneness[57], which would have been *"Wāḥid Wāḥid,"* to the higher level of witnessing Allah's Unique Oneness. He saw the Signs of his Creator everywhere he turned.

When a Muslim leaves the forbidden completely and eliminates all bad behaviors from his character, at that time he will be able to taste the sweetness of faith, *Īmān.* Whoever has purified his self is advancing towards the Station of *Iḥsān,* perfection of character.

When we reach that level of *Iḥsān,* Allah ﷻ calls on us:

وَاذْكُر رَّبَّكَ فِي نَفْسِكَ تَضَرُّعاً وَخِيفَةً وَدُونَ الْجَهْرِ مِنَ الْقَوْلِ بِالْغُدُوِّ وَالآصَالِ وَلاَ تَكُن مِّنَ الْغَافِلِينَ

> *And do (O reader!) bring your Lord to remembrance in your (very) soul, with humility and in reverence, without loudness in words, in the mornings and evenings, and be not of those who are unheedful.*[58]

At this point, there is no more illness in the heart of the seeker. There is only good behavior and reminders of obedience. At this time, he is able to remember his Lord and mention Him *"with humility and in reverence"*—with true emotion and sincere neediness. The seeker mentions Him in the

---

[55]Aḥad is one of the attributes of God defined as the Unique One.

[56]In Arabic, this is known as the Station of *Aḥadīyya.*

[57]In Arabic, this is known as the Station of *Waḥdānīyya.*

[58]Sūratu 'l-ʿArāf [The Heights], 7:205.

morning and in the evening, calling upon his Lord and yearning for obedience to Him throughout his daily life and throughout the night.

THE METHODS OF TRAINING AND PURIFICATION OF THE SELF

1. STUDY WITH A TEACHER

وكان النبي صلى الله عليه وسلم يعرض القرآن في رمضان على جبريل عليه السلام، فكان يدارسه القرآن

On the authority of Ibn 'Abbās: Jibrīl used to meet the Prophet every night in Ramadan and used to study Qur'ān with him.[59]

This *Sunnah* proves the necessity of studying with a teacher. A qualified master is one who has already trod the path of spiritual development, who knows its ins and outs, its opportunities and pitfalls. He or she has already a veteran of the many battles required to defeat the ego and build up the heart and soul. Such a teacher knows the most effective times and places for spiritual training. A true master knows the efficacy of the verses of the Holy Qur'ān in building spiritual power, eliminating spiritual diseases and opening the heart to Allah's Divine Light. Such teachers are able to share these understandings with their students, who are in turn able to take benefit from their company. The time they spend with their teacher will allow these students to more easily purify themselves and advance more quickly on the spiritual path. Left to their own devices, these students might deviate from the *Shari'ah* or otherwise fall into error. The teacher can direct them so that their spiritual training and practices is accordance with the Divine Law, for whatever does not conform to the Shari'ah is false spirituality.

---

[59]Bukhārī.

Allah ﷻ said in the Holy Qur'ān:

يَا أَيُّهَا الَّذِينَ آمَنُواْ اتَّقُواْ اللّهَ وَكُونُواْ مَعَ الصَّادِقِينَ

O you who believe! Fear Allah and keep company with those who are truthful.[60]

Allah's Ancient Words are for all time, ongoing commandments from which we understand the importance of keeping company with the trustworthy. Allah ﷻ orders us to accompany them, because in doing so we see how they live—how they deal with people, how they address their companions, how they relate with their family and even how they deal with opponents—we see how they eat, sleep and drink, and how they worship based on the *Sunnah* of the Best of Creation ﷺ. By accompanying them, one learns all their good manners, perfections and ways of life. It is rare to find someone living their life in such accordance with the Straight Path. Not everyone can do it, but we can all find such a trustworthy one and accompany him or her in order that we may be guided aright.

1.A CONDITIONS FOR BEING A SPIRITUAL TEACHER

The conditions for being a teacher of spiritual discipline are rigorous:

a. The shaykh must be deeply imbued with the knowledge of the religion, both external and esoteric.
b. He must inherit from the Prophet ﷺ and all his predecessors the ability and Divine Support to guide his followers in the externals of the religion and its inner realities.
c. He must be a scholar, well-versed in all religious obligations, such as the conditions of prescribed prayers, fasting, *zakāt* and hajj.
d. He must be knowledgeable in Islamic jurisprudence and all necessary matters of the Divine Law.
e. He must be a scholar in the science of monotheism and all the other conditions of faith.
f. He must have the knowledge of the conditions of the state of excellence.

---

[60] Sūratu 't-Tawbah [Repentance], 9:119.

g. He must have already purified and sanctified himself as a seeker under a guide of his own. Thus, he will have come to know the different stages of the ego, its illnesses and its defects. The guide must be fully aware of all the methods Satan uses to enter the breast and know all the ways to sanctify others and the methods to heal his followers in order to raise them up to the state of perfection.
h. The shaykh must have authorization from his teacher to train his followers, authorization that must extend through a lineage of teachers all the way back to the Prophet ﷺ. As the wise person will not go to a doctor who has no license in healing, so the seeker in this way must find a perfect guide who has received the license, the permission, from his shaykh.

يا ابن عمر ، دينك ، دينك ، إنما هو لحمك ودمك ، فانظر عمن تأخذ ، خذ الدين عن الذين استقاموا ، ولا تأخذ عن الذين قالوا

The Prophet ﷺ said:

O Ibn ʿUmar, your religion is your flesh and blood. Look at those from whom you take your religion. Take it from those who are on the right path and do not take from those who have deviated.[61]

إن هذا العلم دين فانظروا عمن تأخذون دينكم

And the Prophet ﷺ said:

This great knowledge (the knowledge of the self) is by itself the religion, so you have to know from whom you take your religion.[62]

العلماء ورثة الأنبياء

Most importantly, the Prophet ﷺ said:

The scholars of knowledge are the inheritors of the Prophets.

Ibn Khaldūn has mentioned this as one of the proofs for the necessity of following a *shaykh* in the sciences of *taṣawwuf* where he says: "To be in no need of the heir amounts to being in no need of the Prophet."[63]

---

[61] Ḥāfiẓ ibn ʿAlī, *Kanz al-ʿummāl*. Ad-Daylamī in *Musnad al-Firdaws*.
[62] Al-Ḥākim in his *Mustadrak*.
[63] Ibn Khaldūn, *Shifā' al-sā'il li tahdhīb al-masā'il* (Chapter six, on following a Sufi shaykh).

2. REMEMBRANCE OF ALLAH

The fundamental practice of self-purification is *dhikrullāh,* or the remembrance of Allah ﷻ. The purpose of this remembrance is to keep the heart awake by mentioning His Names.

In the Holy Qur'ān, there are more than 190 verses in which *dhikrullāh* is mentioned. Here we relate a representative few:

وَاذْكُر رَّبَّكَ فِي نَفْسِكَ تَضَرُّعاً وَخِيفَةً وَدُونَ الْجَهْرِ مِنَ الْقَوْلِ بِالْغُدُوِّ وَالآصَالِ وَلاَ تَكُن مِّنَ الْغَافِلِينَ

And do thou (O Muhammad) remember your Lord within yourself humbly and with awe, below your breath, at morn and evening, and be not of the neglectful.[64]

يَا أَيُّهَا الَّذِينَ آمَنُوا اذْكُرُوا اللَّهَ ذِكْرًا كَثِيرًا

O you who believe! Remember Allah with much remembrance.[65]

فَاذْكُرُونِي أَذْكُرْكُمْ وَاشْكُرُواْ لِي وَلاَ تَكْفُرُونِ

Therefore remember Me, I will remember you. Give thanks to Me, and reject Me not.[66]

إِنَّمَا الْمُؤْمِنُونَ الَّذِينَ إِذَا ذُكِرَ اللهُ وَجِلَتْ قُلُوبُهُمْ وَإِذَا تُلِيَتْ عَلَيْهِمْ آيَاتُهُ زَادَتْهُمْ إِيمَانًا وَعَلَى رَبِّهِمْ يَتَوَكَّلُونَ

They only are the (true) believers whose hearts feel fear when Allah is mentioned, and when the revelations of Allah are recited unto them they increase their faith, and who trust in their Lord. [67]

The value of *dhikrullāh* is also mentioned in the *ḥadīth*:

وعن عبد الله بن بشر رضي الله عنه أن رجلا قال: يا رسول الله، إن شرائع الإسلام قد كثرت علي، فأخبرني بشيء أتشبث به قال: "لا يزال لسانك رطبًا من ذكر الله".

Someone came to the Prophet ﷺ and asked, "O Messenger of Allah, I am finding that all these different rules of the religion are too difficult. Please give

[64]Sūratu 'l-'Arāf [The Heights], 7:205.
[65]Sūratu 'l-Aḥzāb [The Confederates] 33:41.
[66]Sūratu 'l-Baqara [The Heifer], 2:152.
[67]Sūratu 'l-Anfāl [The Spoils], 8:2.

me something easy that I may accomplish." The Prophet ﷺ answered, "Make your tongue moist with the Remembrance of Allah."[68]

In most verses, what is meant by the word *"dhikr"* is glorifying, exalting, and praising Allah ﷻ and sending salutations upon the Prophet ﷺ. It is important to note that the Holy Qur'ān does not only speak of the benefits of this practice; it also warns against neglecting it:

أَفَمَن شَرَحَ اللَّهُ صَدْرَهُ لِلْإِسْلَامِ فَهُوَ عَلَىٰ نُورٍ مِّن رَّبِّهِ فَوَيْلٌ لِّلْقَاسِيَةِ قُلُوبُهُم مِّن ذِكْرِ اللَّهِ أُولَٰئِكَ فِي ضَلَالٍ مُّبِينٍ

Could, then, one whose bosom Allah has opened wide with willingness towards self-surrender unto Him, so that he is illumined by a light [that flows] from his Sustainer, [be likened to the blind and deaf of heart]? Woe, then, unto those whose hearts are hardened against all remembrance of Allah! They are most obviously lost in error! [69]

2.A BENEFITS OF *DHIKR*

Dhikrullāh is a means—one of many, but among the most important—to accumulate different powers of the self, *jamiʿ ṭāqata 'n-nafs*. These energies are derived from the light with which Allah ﷻ fills the hearts of sincere believers that we mentioned earlier. These energies are accumulated by means of *dhikrullāh,* and they are what allow the seeker to rend the veils that separate him from His Lord, granting him the power of true vision and making his heart a receiver for the Divine Emanations. The master is able to teach the seeker to keep this remembrance constant, so that the heart and tongue are always occupied with it *dhikrullāh.*

ومن فوائد الذكر أيضاً ما ذكره ابن القيم رحمه الله:

أن دور الجنة تُبنى بالذكر، فإذا أمسك الذاكر عن الذكر أمسكت الملائكة عن البناء، وأن الذكر سد بين العبد وبين جهنم فإذا كانت له إلى جهنم طريق عمل من الأعمال، كان الذكر سداً في تلك الطريق، وأن الملائكة تستغفر للذاكر كما تستغفر للتائب، وأن الجبال والقفار تتباهى وتستبشر بمن

[68] Aḥmad, Tirmidhī, Ibn Mājah, and Ibn Ḥibbān (*ḥasan*).

[69] Sūratu 'z-Zumar [The Groups], 39:22.

يذكر الله عز وجل عليها، وأن كثرة ذكر الله عز وجل أمان من النفاق، فإن المنافقين قليلو الذكر لله عز وجل.
قال تبارك وتعالى في المنافقين: " وَلا يَذْكُرُونَ اللّهَ إِلا قَلِيلا " وأن للذكر من بين الأعمال لذة لا يُشبهها شيء فلو لم يكن للعبد من ثوابه إلا اللذة الحاصلة للذاكر، وأنه يكسو الوجة نضرة في الدنيا ونوراً في الآخرة،

Ibn Qayyim said:

Indeed the ground floor of Paradise is built upon *dhikr*. So when the one remembering Allah stops his *dhikr* the angels stop building [the ground floor of Paradise for that servant]. And *dhikr* is truly a barrier between the servant and Hell, such that even if he is on the path to Hell because of some of his deeds, [his] dhikrullāh stands as a barrier in that path and verily the angels ask forgiveness for the one remembering Allah just as they do for the penitent. And verily the mountains and the plains boast and rejoice over one who remembers Allah Exalted upon their surface. And verily excessive Remembrance of Allah ﷻ is security from hypocrisy (nifāq), for verily the hypocrites are those who remember Allah infrequently. Allah ﷻ said regarding the hypocrites, "and they do not remember Allah except a little."[70]

He also said:

And indeed Allah's remembrance obligates Allah ﷻ and His angels to bless the one remembering.

Ibn Qayyim also said:

Surely there is a rapturous pleasure to *dhikr* among all the praiseworthy actions that nothing else resembles, such that if the servant got nothing from his *dhikr* except that ecstasy that comes to the one remembering [it would suffice him], and truly he will be dressed with a shining face in this life and with light in the Hereafter.[71]

---

[70]Sūratu 'n-Nisā [Women], 4:142.

[71]Cited by 'Abdu 'l-'Azīz ibn Muḥammad Salmān in *Manāhil al-hisān fī durūs Ramaḍān.*

2.B THE FLAME OF THE HEART

وَمَن لَّمْ يَجْعَلِ اللهُ لَهُ نُورًا فَمَا لَهُ مِن نُّورٍ

For any to whom Allah gives not light, there is no light! [72]

When a heart is constant in remembrance it becomes illumined with a flame that always burns brightly. The strength of that flame depends on how much the seeker engages in *dhikrullāh*. When that flame appears in the heart, he is able to weigh right and wrong, discerning the good from the bad. This flame also grants contentment with everything that Allah ﷻ gives, causing anger to subside.

There is difference between soul and spirit, *rūḥ wa ʿn-nafs*. The heart is the house of the soul. The spirit permeates the entire body in much the same way the nervous system does. It commands the whole body. When the soul is energized by *dhikrullāh*, that flame will expand throughout the entire body and the nervous system giving it the power to accept every condition and situation. As that flame grows, it overtakes the whole body and that person becomes truly pious and sincere. Thus, the soul and the spirit come together.

This happened to Sayyidina Khiḍr:

فَوَجَدَا عَبْدًا مِّنْ عِبَادِنَا آتَيْنَاهُ رَحْمَةً مِنْ عِندِنَا وَعَلَّمْنَاهُ مِن لَّدُنَّا عِلْمًا

They two found one of our servants that We had taught from our heavenly knowledge[73]

2.C THE VISION OF THE PURIFIED HEART

القلب بيت الرب

It is related that the Prophet ﷺ said: "The heart is the House of the Lord."[74]

How is this possible? Because this heart becomes vast through the power of remembrance of Allah's Names and Attributes. When the spirit and the soul come together, the spirit will become stronger. In this way, the

---

[72]Sūratu 'n-Nūr [The Light], 24:40.

[73]Sūratu 'l-Kahf [The Cave], 18:65.

[74]Ibn Mājah relates a longer wording with a similar meaning.

veils that separate the seeker from his Lord are rent and the heart is able to perceive that which cannot be seen with the eyes, as described in *Ḥadīth Qudsī*:

وعن أبي هريرة قال قال رسول الله صلى الله عليه وسلم إن الله تعالى قال من عادى لي وليا فقد آذنته بالحرب وما تقرب إلي عبدي بشيء أحب إلي مما افترضت عليه وما يزال عبدي يتقرب إلي بالنوافل حتى أحبه فإذا أحببته كنت سمعه الذي يسمع به وبصره الذي يبصر به ويده التي يبطش بها ورجله التي يمشي بها وإن سألني لأعطينه ولئن استعاذني لأعيذنه وما ترددت عن شيء أنا فاعله ترددي عن نفس المؤمن يكره الموت وأنا أكره مساءته ولا بد له منه . رواه البخاري .

My servant continues to approach Me through voluntary worship until I love him. And when I love him I will be the ears with which he hears, I will be the eyes with which he sees; I will be the tongue with which he speaks, I will be the hand with which he acts, and I will be the foot with which he walks.[75]

Another *ḥadīth* states:

اتقوا فراسة المؤمن، فإنه ينظر بنور الله عز وجل

The Prophet ﷺ said, "*Beware of the vision of a sincere believer for verily he sees with the Light of Allah.*"[76]

This refers to the special vision that is granted to the sincere servant. An example of this is found in the story of Sayyidina 'Umar ؓ:

ولابن مردويه عن ابن عمر عن أبيه أنه كان يخطب يوم الجمعة فعرض في خطبته أن قال: يا سارية الجبل! من استرعى الذئب ظلم. فالتفت الناس بعضهم لبعض، فقال لهم علي: ليخرجن مما قال. فلما فرغ سألوه فقال: وقع في خلدي أن المشركين هزموا إخواننا، وأنهم يمرون بجبل فإن عدلوا إليه قاتلوا من وجه واحد، وإن جاوزوا هلكوا، فخرج مني ما تزعمون أنكم سمعتموه. فجاء البشير بعد شهر وذكر أنهم سمعوا صوت عمر في ذلك اليوم. قال: فعدلنا إلى الجبل ففتح الله علينا. قال في اللآلئ: وقد أفرد الحافظ القطب الحلبي لطرقه جزءا، ووثق رجال هذه الطريق. وقال: ذكره ابن عساكر وابن ماكولا وغيرهم، وسارية له صحبة

---

[75] Bukhārī and Muslim.
[76] Narrated by Imām at-Tirmidhī in his book of *Tafsīr* on the authority of ibn Sa'īd al-Ḥākim. Al-Bukhārī in his *Tārīkh*, aṭ-Ṭabarānī in his *Kabīr* and Ibn 'Adi in his *Kāmil* from Ibn 'Umar.

Ibn 'Umar ⁂ said that his father, Sayyidina 'Umar ⁂, was delivering a sermon on Friday. In the middle of his sermon, he shouted, "Ya Sārīyyah, al-jabal! O Sārīyyah! [look towards] the mountain!" Then he resumed his sermon...Some people looked at each other in dismay. Sayyidina 'Alī ⁂ said to them, "He will likely say (something) about this statement." When the people had finished the prayer, they asked Sayyidina 'Umar ⁂ about the incident. He said, "The idea crossed my mind that the enemy aggressors had defeated our brothers and they would run towards the mountain. Thus, if the Muslims moved towards the mountain, they would have to fight on one side only, while if they advanced, they would be destroyed. So those words escaped my mouth." After a month, a messenger came with good news. He said, "The people of the army heard Sayyidina 'Umar's ⁂ voice on that day. We all went towards the mountain and Allah made us victorious."[77]

That miracle (*karāmah*) was a sign that Sayyidina 'Umar ⁂ had two characteristics from true faith: The Reality of Hearing, *'Ilmu 'l-Yaqīn* and the Reality of Seeing, *'Aynu 'l-Yaqīn*. The first characteristic is like one that Allah ⁂ gave to Sārīyya⁂ and his troops from His Divine Attribute the Hearer, as-Samʿi. But Sayyidina 'Umar ⁂ also could see what was occurring through the Reality of Certainty, *Haqqu 'l-Yaqīn*. Sārīyya⁂ and his troops were only able to hear from afar. They could not see Sayyidina 'Umar ⁂, whereas Sayyidina 'Umar ⁂ was seeing, hearing and speaking across the vast distance from Madina to Shām.[ii]

3. CONTEMPLATION ON ALLAH'S PRESENCE

Thus, the practice of *dhikrullāh* strengthens faith and develops the power of true vision, allowing the seeker to advance to the practice of *murāqabatillāh fī 's-sirr w 'al-ʿalānīyya*, to be able to meditate and focus upon Allah ⁂, whether alone or in a crowd. This is important, for He said in the Holy Qur'ān:

---

[77]Ibn ʿAsākir, Ibn Makūlan, Ibn al-Mardawayh and other narrations by al-Bayhaqī in *Dalā'il an-nubuwwah*, al-Lalakaʾī in *Sharḥ as-sunnah*, and al-Waqidī with variant wordings.

أَلَمْ تَرَ أَنَّ اللَّهَ يَعْلَمُ مَا فِي السَّمَاوَاتِ وَمَا فِي الْأَرْضِ مَا يَكُونُ مِن نَّجْوَى ثَلَاثَةٍ إِلَّا هُوَ رَابِعُهُمْ وَلَا خَمْسَةٍ
إِلَّا هُوَ سَادِسُهُمْ وَلَا أَدْنَى مِن ذَلِكَ وَلَا أَكْثَرَ إِلَّا هُوَ مَعَهُمْ أَيْنَ مَا كَانُوا ثُمَّ يُنَبِّئُهُم بِمَا عَمِلُوا يَوْمَ
الْقِيَامَةِ إِنَّ اللَّهَ بِكُلِّ شَيْءٍ عَلِيمٌ

Do you not see that Allah knows (all) that is in the Heavens and on Earth? There is not a secret consultation between three but He makes the fourth among them, nor between five but He makes the sixth, nor between fewer nor more but He is in their midst, wheresoever they be. In the end will He tell them the truth of their conduct on the Day of Judgment, for Allah has full knowledge of all things. [78]

Allah ﷻ also said:

الَّذِينَ يَذْكُرُونَ اللَّهَ قِيَامًا وَقُعُودًا وَعَلَى جُنُوبِهِمْ وَيَتَفَكَّرُونَ فِي خَلْقِ السَّمَاوَاتِ وَالْأَرْضِ رَبَّنَا مَا خَلَقْتَ
هَذا بَاطِلاً سُبْحَانَكَ فَقِنَا عَذَابَ النَّارِ

Those that remember Allah, standing, sitting, and on their sides contemplating about the creation of the Heavens and the Earth (and say): Our Lord! You did not create this in vain. Glory be to You! Preserve us from the torment of Fire.[79]

أَوَلَمْ يَنظُرُواْ فِي مَلَكُوتِ السَّمَاوَاتِ وَالأَرْضِ وَمَا خَلَقَ اللَّهُ مِن شَيْءٍ وَأَنْ عَسَى أَن يَكُونَ قَدِ اقْتَرَبَ
أَجَلُهُمْ فَبِأَيِّ حَدِيثٍ بَعْدَهُ يُؤْمِنُونَ

Have they not considered the dominion of the Heavens and the Earth, and what things Allah has created, and that it may be that their own term draws nigh? In what fact after this will they believe?[80]

قُلِ انظُرُواْ مَاذَا فِي السَّمَاوَاتِ وَالأَرْضِ وَمَا تُغْنِي الآيَاتُ وَالنُّذُرُ عَن قَوْمٍ لاَّ يُؤْمِنُونَ

Say: Behold what is in the Heavens and the Earth! But revelations and warnings avail not folk who will not believe. [81]

---

[78]Sūratu 'l-Mujādilah [The Disputant], 58:7.
[79] Sūrat Āli-'Imrān [The Family of 'Imrān], 3:191.
[80]Sūratu 'l-'Arāf [The Heights], 7:185.
[81] Sūrah Yūnus [Jonah], 10: 101.

وَكَأَيِّن مِّنْ آيَةٍ فِي السَّمَاوَاتِ وَالْأَرْضِ يَمُرُّونَ عَلَيْهَا وَهُمْ عَنْهَا مُعْرِضُونَ

How many a portent is there in the Heavens and the Earth that they pass by with face averted![82]

أَفَلَمْ يَسِيرُوا فِي الْأَرْضِ فَتَكُونَ لَهُمْ قُلُوبٌ يَعْقِلُونَ بِهَا أَوْ آذَانٌ يَسْمَعُونَ بِهَا
فَإِنَّهَا لَا تَعْمَى الْأَبْصَارُ وَلَٰكِن تَعْمَى الْقُلُوبُ الَّتِي فِي الصُّدُورِ

Have they not traveled in the land, and have they hearts wherewith to feel and ears wherewith to hear? For indeed it is not the eyes that grow blind, but it is the hearts that are within the bosoms, that grow blind.[83]

Tafakkur is worship based on contemplation of Allah's creation. It involves observing the Earth, the Sun, the planets, the stars and the Moon; observing the trees, the plants, and the animals; observing the seasons and their transition from one to another. One observes the perfect cycles of water, air and energy; the perfection of the protection afforded by Earth's atmosphere, ionosphere and magnetosphere from harmful rays, meteors and energy. One observes the ants and bees, and the different ways they live and work together with intricate organization and determination. One observes the elephants, whales, birds, insects, contemplating their lives and biological diversity. One observes the microscopic world of bacteria and viruses and the still smaller world of molecular and atomic structures in their incredible miniscule perfection.

As the seeker contemplates these wonders, he comes to the full realization that all are His amazing creation and is thereby able to authentically appreciate Allah's Oneness and Greatness. This allows the seeker to progress even deeper in his meditation, to realize the importance of keeping his heart connected to the Divine Presence and to advance even farther on his spiritual journey. In this way, he becomes an individual who is sincere in the depths of his belief and to the core of his heart. His life becomes a constant meditation on the Divine that transports him from the abyss of the ego to the deep oceans of Allah's Remembrance.

---

[82] Sūrah Yūsuf [Joseph], 12:105.

[83] Sūratu 'l-Ḥajj [The Pilgrimage], 22:46.

Many verses of the Holy Qur'ān encourage this practice of contemplation, and *tafakkur* is further mentioned in many *ḥadīth* of the Prophet ﷺ. Indeed, there are seventeen verses in the Qur'ān that explicitly use the verb *tafakkar*. There are seventy-nine other verses containing the root *"fakara"*, to think or reason, and there are countless others that speak of those who have eyes, *ulī 'l-abṣār*, understanding, *ulī 'l-albāb*, and reasoning, *ulī 'n-nuhā*.[84] Moreover, eighteen verses ask if we "see not" (*alam yaraw, afalam yaraw, awalam yaraw*), instructing us to observe Allah's creation, generally or specifically, and take heed from these observations. There are 120 verses that ask the reader or listener if he knows (from the root: *'alama*).

Such observation allows us to remain mindful of the Presence of Allah, *murāqabah,* allowing us to truly feel that He is nearer than our jugular vein, nearer to us than our own selves.

There was a spiritual teacher who told all his students: "Go slaughter a chicken where no one can see you." And so they did, each returning to inform their teacher of their accomplishment save one who did not return. When the teacher found him, he asked what had happened. The student said, "How can I slaughter the chicken where no one can see me? Allah ﷻ is seeing me; the Prophet ﷺ is seeing me and my teacher is seeing me."

4. THE NIGHT VIGIL

Following the first revelation of Surat al-'Alaq, Allah ﷻ revealed:

يَا أَيُّهَا الْمُزَّمِّلُ قُمِ اللَّيْلَ إِلَّا قَلِيلًا نِصْفَهُ أَوِ انقُصْ مِنْهُ قَلِيلًا أَوْ زِدْ عَلَيْهِ وَرَتِّلِ الْقُرْآنَ تَرْتِيلًا إِنَّا سَنُلْقِي عَلَيْكَ قَوْلًا ثَقِيلًا

O you, folded in garments! Stand (in prayer) by night, but not all night, half of it or a little less or a little more, and recite the Qur'ān in slow, measured rhythmic tones. Soon shall We send down to you a weighty Message. Truly

---

[84]*Ulī 'l-abṣār,* "those who have eyes." Sūrat Āli-'Imrān [The Family of 'Imrān], 3:13; Sūratu 'n-Nūr [The Light], 24:44; *ulī 'l-albāb,* "those endowed with understanding." Sūrah Ṣād, 38:43; Sūratu 'z-Zumar [The Groups], 39:21; Sūrah Ghāfir, 40:54; Sūrat Āli-'Imrān, 3:190; Sūrah Yūsuf [Joseph], 12:111. *ūli 'n-nuhā,* "those who are endowed with reason." Sūrah ṬāḤā, 20:54; Sūrah ṬāḤā, 20:128.

the rising by night is most potent for governing (the soul) and most suitable for (framing) the Word (of Prayer and Praise).[85]

Allah ﷻ wanted the Prophet ﷺ to be constant in meditation and remembrance of his Lord. That is extremely difficult to do late at night when everyone is sleeping, but this is also a most efficacious time for worship as the above verse makes clear.

Waking up for night worship requires a major struggle against the ego. Thus, the seeker is encouraged to wake up and pray *Ṣalāt at-tahajjud,* the night prayer, in order to learn patience and obedience and to accompany teachers who have been practicing that discipline and trying their best to eliminate their bad characteristics and bad manners.

5. WORSHIP AND OBEDIENCE

True servanthood is based on *al-ʿibādāt wa 't-taʿat,* worship and obedience. As the seeker ascends through different levels of unveiling, he begins to realize that the only way to approach His Lord is through worship, for Allah ﷻ said:

قَدْ أَفْلَحَ مَن تَزَكَّى وَذَكَرَ اسْمَ رَبِّهِ فَصَلَّى

The one who attains a higher level of purification will have succeeded And remembers the name of his Lord, so prays.[86]

Let us examine this verse more closely. In it, Allah ﷻ says that, as the seeker attains to higher and higher levels, he comes to the sincere remembrance of his Lord's Name. This demonstrates that the real and authentic remembrance of Allah ﷻ is only possible once the self is purified. The one who has done this is able to truly remember his Lord, not just imitate that remembrance. The verse goes on to state *"so [he] prays."* This means that such an enlightened person feels the reality of the Divine Presence at every moment when he is performing the obligatory five prayers. From these he seeks further closeness by observing the *nawāfil,* voluntary worship.

---

[85]Sūratu 'l-Muzzammil [The Enshrouded One], 73:1-6.
[86]Sūratu 'l-ʿAlā [The Most High], 87:14.

Even today, there are among the practitioners of this science those who in every moment go and make ablution, then come and pray two *raka'ats sunnat al-wuḍū*, then in five minutes repeat it again. They want to feel that they are doing more voluntary worship, because they know that it is pleasing to Allah, because:

الوضوء على الوضوء نور على نور

The Prophet ﷺ said, "Ablution over ablution is 'light upon light.'"[87]

Such people fall under Allah's Words that he has already mentioned: "My servant continues to approach Me through voluntary worship until I love him ..." Such a person becomes a subtle being who can direct others to what is correct and what is not, what is sickness and what is health.

6. GROUP REMEMBRANCE

Another important practice is to perform *dhikrullāh* in a group, forming circles such as those mentioned by Ibn Qayyim, who said:

> And verily, whoever wishes to inhabit the Gardens of Paradise in this life should become a member of the gatherings of *dhikr*, for verily they are the Gardens of Paradise and verily the gatherings of *dhikr* are the gatherings of angels.

When people attend associations of *dhikrullāh*, they hear recitation of the Qur'ān in beautiful voices and melodies, the most beautiful praising of the Prophet ﷺ and with the *dhikrullāh* angels surround them, as mentioned in the *ḥadīth*. This is how the Prophet ﷺ was listening to the Holy Qur'ān, in a melodious way. He also used to listen to such praising and poetry by Ḥassān ibn Thābit, the likes of which made tears fall and left the listener wanting nothing from this life.

---

[87]Razzīn in his *Musnad*.

7. ABSTINENCE

Zuhd, abstinence, is to throw *dunyā* from the heart. This does not necessarily require eliminating *dunyā* from one's life, rather it requires the seeker to through it from his heart.

ورب غني شاكر أفضل من فقير صابر،

For that reason it is said, "It may be that a thankful wealthy person is better than a patient pauper." [88]

He who possesses little worships like the wealthy, but a pious wealthy person both worships and gives charity. For someone who has truly eliminated love of wealth from his heart, possession of great wealth will not create the disease of attachment. Instead, he will spend it in Allah's Way. The use of wealth in Allah's Way may be better by hundreds and thousands of times than a patient pauper's worship.

With the simultaneous accumulation of all positive character traits and the elimination of all negative ones, the seeker's heart begins to fill with the power needed to overcome all evil inclinations, for Allah ﷻ said:

وَالَّذِينَ جَاهَدُوا فِينَا لَنَهْدِيَنَّهُمْ سُبُلَنَا وَإِنَّ اللهَ لَمَعَ الْمُحْسِنِينَ

And those who strive in Our (cause), We will certainly guide them to our Paths for verily Allah is with those who do right.[89]

This means that when we struggle against the inclinations of our lower self, Allah ﷻ will show us the way to leave those bad characteristics and behaviors behind us. Those who are accumulating pure spiritual energy will be guided in the ways that Allah ﷻ wants for them, and by means of this guidance they will reach what Allah ﷻ wants for them. Such persons are described in the Holy Qur'ān:

مِنَ الْمُؤْمِنِينَ رِجَالٌ صَدَقُوا مَا عَاهَدُوا اللهَ عَلَيْهِ فَمِنْهُم مَّن قَضَى نَحْبَهُ وَمِنْهُم مَّن يَنتَظِرُ وَمَا بَدَّلُوا تَبْدِيلًا

---

[88]A saying of Abū Abbās al-'Atā.
[89]Sūratu 'l-'Ankabūt [The Spider], 29:69.

Among the Believers are men who have been true to their covenant with Allah. Of them some have completed their vow (to the extreme), and some (still) wait: but they have never changed (their determination) in the least.[90]

These purified ones do what Allah ﷻ wants with full knowledge of the covenant made before this worldly life, when we were in the world of souls, on the Day of Vows and Binding Promises (*Yawm al-ʿAhdi wa 'l-Mīthāq*).

8. SECLUSION

The scholars of Islam realized the importance of seclusion by studying the life of the Prophet ﷺ, and they came to understand its necessity in the spiritual journey of the seeker. That is why they made their hearts to be remote from *dunyā*.

Recall how the Prophet ﷺ used to retreat to Ghāri Hirā for many months of the year to worship and contemplate in order to be able to receive heavenly knowledge.

Allah ﷻ said:

إِنَّا سَنُلْقِي عَلَيْكَ قَوْلًا ثَقِيلًا

Soon shall We send down to thee a weighty Message. [91]

Allah ﷻ guided the Prophet ﷺ to prepare himself in Ghāri Hirā, to guide him in his spiritual life in order that one day he would be ready to receive that heavenly revelation. Allah ﷻ also said in the Holy Qur'ān:

لَوْ أَنزَلْنَا هَٰذَا الْقُرْآنَ عَلَىٰ جَبَلٍ لَّرَأَيْتَهُ خَاشِعًا مُّتَصَدِّعًا مِّنْ خَشْيَةِ اللَّهِ وَتِلْكَ الْأَمْثَالُ نَضْرِبُهَا لِلنَّاسِ لَعَلَّهُمْ يَتَفَكَّرُونَ

Had We sent down this Qur'ān on a mountain, verily you would have seen it humble itself and cleave asunder for fear of Allah! Such are the similitudes that We propound to men that they may reflect.[92]

---

[90]Sūratu 'l-Aḥzāb [The Confederates], 33:23.
[91]Sūratu 'l-Muzammil, [The Enshrouded One], 73:5.
[92]Sūratu 'l-Ḥashr [The Gathering], 59:21.

If this revelation would have shattered a mountain, imagine what it would have done to a human being. Therefore, Allah ﷻ prepared His Prophet ﷺ through spiritual purification, *Tazkīyyat an-Nafs,* in the cave, and it was there that His Revelation finally came down. It did not come down in the Prophet's house, or in the Sacred Mosque, or in a seminar, or in worship. Revelation came only in a cave after the Prophet ﷺ had completely secluded himself from worldly life. The first revelation was *"Iqrā! Read in the Name of your Lord."* Later, after the Prophet ﷺ had built up his spirituality through Allah's Guidance, Allah ﷻ allowed him to receive revelation in "normal" circumstances. Yet, despite this and despite the fact that by the end of his earthly life he was leader of a great nation, the Prophet ﷺ continued to observe seclusion, and he remained *zāhid,* ascetic and humble in his means, until the day of his passing.

Conclusion

The life of every human being is a struggle between good and evil. We have seen that the externalities of our religion are alone insufficient to grant us victory over the same evil impulses that inspired Cain to raise his hand against his brother. Rather, we must add to these the practices of the science of self-purification in order to cleanse our hearts and rid ourselves of these diseases of the spirit. Only then can we ensure that good will triumph over evil within us.

The Imāms of our pure religion cautioned against the mere thirst for knowledge at the expense of training the ego and purifying it of lust and desire for material wealth. Imām Ghazālī left the halls of learning in the midst of a prestigious career in order to devote himself to self-purification out of concern for his own soul, at the outset of which he wrote his magisterial *Iḥyā 'Ulum al-dīn* that begins with a warning to those who consider religion to consist merely in *fiqh* or jurisprudence.

Heed the words of Imām adh-Dhahabī:

> Today in our time, the quest for knowledge and *ḥādīth* no longer requires of the *ḥādīth* scholar the obligation of living up to it; that is the goal of *ḥādīth*: pursuing the study of *ḥādīth* is other than the *ḥādīth* itself.[93]

This warning stands stronger than ever today, for while thousands of young men and women run to study Islamic theology and *fiqh*, it is only a few who seek a teacher who will train them in application of this book learning and guide them along the path of self-purification that allows them to truly live it. It is for the purpose of "the *ḥādīth* itself", for the purpose of living up to the *Sunnah* of the Prophet ﷺ whose manners were the Holy Qur'ān, according to the well-known *ḥādīth* of 'Ā'isha ﵂, that the great masters of self-purification gave up the pursuit of worldly allurements, and placed above it the acquisition of *Iḥsān* or perfect character.

---

[93]Dhahabī as cited in Sakhāwī, *al-Jawāhir wa al-durar fī tarjamat shaykh al-islām Ibn Ḥajar* (al-'Asqalani), ed. Ḥamīd 'Abd al-Mājid and ṬāḤā al-Zaynī (Cairo: Wizārat al-awqāf, al-majlis al-a'la li al-shu'ūn al-islāmīyya, lajnahiḥyā' al-turāth al-islāmī, 1986) pp. 21-22.

Therefore, it behooves those who today seek a solution to the perennial conflict between good and evil to return to this all-important science of the soul. With it, it is hoped that a change for the better can be affected. When that positive change occurs in the individual, its impact will spread to the level of family, then to the community and finally wider still to the entire nation. We ask Allah ﷻ to give us the guidance and inspiration to implement such a course of study and practice in a short time, for truly He is the Changer of Hearts.

Appendix: What the Scholars of Islam Said about *Tasawwuf*

The following quotations of the scholars of Islamic Divine Law regarding the precedence of the knowledge and science of *Taṣawwuf,* (Purification of the Self) are excerpted from the book *The Naqshbandi Sufi Way: History and Guidebook of the Saints of the Golden Chain.*[94]

IBN TAYMIYYA (661 - 728 A.H.)

التصوف عندهم له حقائق وأحوال معروفة ، قد تكلموا في حدوده وسيرته وأخلاقه كقول بعضهم
: " الصوفي " من صفا من الكدر ، وامتلأ من الفكر ، واستوى عنده الذهب والحجر "
التصوف " : كتمان المعاني ، وترك الدعاوى ، وأشباه ذلك ، وهم يسيرون بالصوفي إلى معنى
: الصديق ، وأفضل الخلق بعد الأنبياء الصديقون ، كما قال الله تعالى
وَمَن يُطِعِ اللّهَ وَالرَّسُولَ فَأُوْلَـئِكَ مَعَ الَّذِينَ أَنْعَمَ اللّهُ عَلَيْهِم مِّنَ النَّبِيِّينَ وَالصِّدِّيقِينَ وَالشُّهَدَاء
وَالصَّالِحِينَ وَحَسُنَ أُولَـئِكَ رَفِيقًا...
والصواب : أنهم مجتهدون في طاعة الله ، كما اجتهد غيرهم من أهل طاعة الله ، فيهم السابق المقرب
بحسب اجتهاده...

Taṣawwuf has realities and states of experience that Sufis talk about in their science. Some of it is that the Sufi is that one who purifies himself from anything that distracts him from the remembrance of Allah and who will be so filled up with knowledge of the heart and knowledge of the mind to the point that the value of gold and stones will be the same to him. And *Taṣawwuf* is safeguarding the precious meanings and leaving behind the call to fame and vanity in order to reach the state of Truthfulness, because the best of humans after the prophets are the *Ṣiddiqīn,* as Allah mentioned them in the verse:

---

[94]Shaykh Muhammad Kabbani, KAZI, 1995.

> *(And all who obey Allah and the Apostle) are in the company of those on whom is the grace of Allah: of the prophets, the sincere lovers of truth, the martyrs and the righteous; Ah! what a beautiful fellowship.*[95]

...The truth is, they are striving in Allah's obedience, as others of Allah's People strove in Allah's obedience. So from them you will find the Foremost in Nearness by virtue of his striving.[96]

The miracles of saints are absolutely true and correct, by the acceptance of all Muslim scholars and the Qur'ān has pointed to it in different places, and the *ḥādīth* of the Prophet ﷺ has mentioned it, and whoever denies the miraculous power of saints are only people who are innovators and their followers.[97]

IMAM ABU HANIFA (85 - 150 A.H.)

.لولا السنتان لهلك النعمان، فقد تتلمذ سنتان في مجلس الامام الصادق

If it were not for two years, I would have perished.

He said, "For two years I accompanied Sayyidina Ja'far aṣ-Ṣādiq and I acquired the spiritual knowledge that made me a gnostic in the Way.[98]

IMAM MALIK (95 - 179 A.H.)

يقول الإمام مالك رحمه الله تعالى :من تفقه ولم يتصوف فقد تفسق، ومن تصوف ولم يتفقه فقد تزندق ومن جمع بينهما فقد تحقق

Whoever studies Jurisprudence [*tafaqaha*] and didn't study Sufism [*taṣawwafa*] will be corrupted; and whoever studied Sufism and didn't study Jurisprudence will becọme a heretic; and whoever combined both will be reach the Truth.[99]

---

[95]Sūratu 'n-Nisā [Women], 4:69.

[96]*Majmu'a Fatāwā Ibn Taymīyya al-Kubrā,* Vol. 11, Book of *Taṣawwuf,* p. 497.

[97]*Al-Mukhtaṣar al-Fatawā,* p. 603.

[98]*Ad-Durr al-Mukhtār,* vol. 1, p. 43.

[99]'Alī al-Adawī , vol. 2, p. 195.

IMAM SHAFI'I (150 - 205 A.H.)

قال الإمام الشافعي رحمه الله تعالى: صحبت الصوفية فاستفدت منهم كلمتين قولهم : الوقت سيف نفسك إن لم تشغلها بالحق شغلتك بالباطل : إن لم تقطعه قطعك وقولهم

I accompanied the Sufis and received from them but three words: their statement that time is a sword: if you do not cut it, it cuts you; their statement that if you do not keep your ego busy with truth it will keep you busy with falsehood; their statement that deprivation is immunity.[100]

IMAM AHMAD BIN HANBAL (164 - 241 A.H.)

كان الإمام أحمد رحمه الله تعالى (قبل مصاحبته للصوفية يقول لولده عبدالله رحمه الله تعالى : (يا ولدي عليك بالحديث وإياك ومجالسة هؤلاء الذين سموا أنفسهم صوفية فإنهم ربما كان أحدهم جاهلا بأحكام دينه فلما صحب أبا حمزةالبغدادي الصوفي وعرف أحوال القوم أصبح يقول لولده: يا ولدي عليك بمجالسة هؤلاء القوم، فإنهم زادوا علينا بكثرة العلم والمراقبة والخشية والزهد وعلو الهمة

O my son, you have to sit with the People of Sufism, because they are like a fountain of knowledge and they keep the Remembrance of Allah in their hearts. they are the ascetics and they have the most spiritual power.[101]

IMAM GHAZALI (450 - 505 A.H.)

ثم إني لما فرغت من هذه العلوم أقبلت بهمتي على طريق الصوفية ،وعلمت أن طريقهم إنما يتم بعلم وعمل، وكان حاصل علمهم قطع عقبات النفس والنزه عن أخلاقها المذمومة وصفاتها الخبيثة حتى يتوصل بذلك إلى تخلية القلب من غير الله تعالى وتحليته بذكر الله

I knew verily that Sufis are the seekers in Allah's Way, and their conduct is the best conduct, and their way is the best way, and their manners are the most sanctified. They have cleaned their hearts from other than Allah and they have made them as pathways for rivers to run receiving knowledge of the Divine Presence.[102]

---

[100]Ibn al-Qayyim in his *Madārij al-sālikīn* (3:128) and al-Ḥāfiẓ as-Suyūṭī in his *Tā'yid al-Ḥaqīqat al-'Alīyya,* p. 15.

[101]Shaykh Amīn al-Kurdī, *Tanwīr al-Qulūb* p. 405.

[102]Īmām Ghazālī, *al-Munqidh min aḍ-ḍallāl,* p. 131.

FAKHR AD-DIN AR-RAZI (544 - 606 A.H.)

والمتصوفة قوم يشتغلون بالفكر وتجرد النفس عن العلائق الجسمانية ويجتهدون أن لا يخلو سرهم وبالهم عن ذكر الله تعالى في سائر تصرفاتهم وأعمالهم

...The way of Sufis for seeking Knowledge, is to disconnect themselves from this worldly life, and they keep themselves constantly busy ...with *dhikrullāh*, in all their actions and behaviors. [103]

IMAM NAWAWI (620 - 676 A.H.)

The specifications of the Way of the Sufis are ... to keep the Presence of Allah in your heart in public and in private; to follow the *Sunnah* of the Prophet ﷺ ... to be happy with what Allah gave you...[104]

IBN KHALDUN (733 - 808 A.H.)

وأصله أن طريقة هؤلاء القوم لم تزل عند سلف الأمة وكبارها من الصحابة والتابعين ومن بعدهم طريقة الحق

The way of the Sufis is the way of the preceding Scholars between the Companions and Predecessors of those who followed good guidance...[105]

TAJUDDIN AS-SUBKI (727 - 771 A.H.)

حياهم الله وبياهم وجمعنا في الجنة نحن وإياهم وقد تشعبت الأقوال فيهم تشعبا ناشئا عن الجهل بحقيقتهم لكثرة المتلبسين بهاإلى أن قال وإنهم المعرضون عن الدنيا المشتغلون في أغلب الأوقات ثم تحدث عن تعاريف التصوف إلى أن قال: والحاصل أنهم أهل الله وخاصته الذين .. بالعبادة ترتجي الرحمة بذكرهم ويستنزل الغيث بدعائهم فرضي الله عنهم وعنا بهم

May Allah praise them [the Sufis] and greet them and may Allah cause us to be with them in Paradise. Too many things have been said about them and too many ignorant people have said things that are not related to them. And the truth is that those people left the world and were busy with worship.

---

[103] Fakhr al-Dīn al-Rāzī, *'Itiqādāt Furāq al-Muslimīn*, pp. 72, 73.
[104] Imām Nawawī, *Maqāsid at-tawḥīd (Letters)*, p. 20.
[105] Ibn Khaldūn, *Muqaddimat ibn al-Khaldūn*, p. 328.

...They are the People of Allah, whose supplications and prayer Allah accepts and by means of whom Allah supports human beings.[106]

JALALUDDIN AS-SUYUTI (849 - 911 A.H.)

إن التصوف في نفسه علم شريف، وإن مداره على اتباع السنة وترك البدع

At-Taṣawwuf in itself is the best and most honorable knowledge. It explains how to follow the *Sunnah* of the Prophet ﷺ and to put aside innovation.[107]

IBN QAYYIM (691 - 751 A.H.)

We can witness the greatness of the People of Sufism, in the eyes of the earliest generations of Muslims by what has been mentioned by Sufyān ath-Thawrī (d. 161 A.H.), one of the greatest imāms of the second century and one of the foremost legal scholars. He said, "If it had not been for Abū Hishām aṣ-Ṣūfī (d. 115) I would never have perceived the action of the subtlest forms of hypocrisy in the self... Among the best of people is the Sufi learned in jurisprudence.[108]

`ABDULLAH IBN MUHAMMAD IBN `ABDUL WAHHAB (1115 - 1201 A.H.)

My father Muḥammad ibn ʿAbdul Wahhāb and I do not deny or criticize the science of Sufism, but on the contrary, we support it because it purifies the external and the internal of the hidden sins that are related to the heart and to the outward form. Even though the individual might externally be on the right way, internally he might be on the wrong way. Sufism is necessary to correct it.[109]

IBN `ABIDIN (1198 - 1252 A.H.)

فهم لايستمعون إلا من الإله ولا يشتاقون إلا له إن ذكروه ناحوا وإن شكروه باحوا وإن وجدوه صاحوا وإن شهدوه استراحوا

---

[106]Tāj al-Dīn as-Subkī, *Muʿīd an-Naʿm*, p. 190, the chapter entitled *"Taṣawwuf"*.

[107]al-Ḥāfiẓ Jalāl al-Dīn as-Suyūṭī, *Tāʾyid al-Ḥaqīqat al-ʿAlīyya*, p. 57.

[108]Ibn Qayyim al-Jawzīyyah, *Manāzil as-Sāʾirīn*.

[109]ibn ʿAbdul Wahhāb, *ad-Diāʿat mukathaffa ḍid ash-shaykh ibn ʿAbdul Wahhāb*, p. 85.

The Seekers in this Sufi Way don't hear except from the Divine Presence and they don't love any but Him. If they remember Him they cry, and if they thank Him they are happy; ... May Allah bless them.[110]

MUHAMMAD `ABDUH (1265 - 1323 A.H.)

Taṣawwuf appeared in the first century of Islam and it received a tremendous honor. It purified the self and straightened the conduct and gave knowledge to people from the Wisdom and Secrets of the Divine Presence.[111]

RASHID RIDA (1282 - 1354 A.H.)

لقد انفرد الصوفية بركن عظيم من أركان الدين، لا يطاولهم فيه مطاول، وهو التهذيب علماً وتخلقاً وتحققاً، ثم لما دونت العلوم في الملة، كتب شيوخ هذه الطائفة في الأخلاق ومحاسبة النفس

Sufism was a unique pillar from the pillars of the religion. Its purpose was to purify the self and to take account of one's daily behavior and to raise the people to a high station of spirituality.[112]

MAULANA ABUL HASAN `ALI AN-NADAWI (1331- 1420 A.H.)

إن هؤلاء الصوفية كانوا يبايعون الناس على التوحيد والإخلاص واتباع السنة والتوبة عن المعاصي والظلم والقسوة ويرغبونهم في التحلي بالأخلاق الحسنة والتخلي عن الرذائل مثل الكبر والحسد والبغضاء واللم وحب الجاه وتزكية النفس وإصلاحها ويعلمونهم ذكر الله والنصح لعباده والقناعة والإيثار وعلاوة على هذه البيعة التي كانت رمز الصلة العميقة الخاصة بين الشيخ ومريديه ، إنهم كانوا يعظون الناس دائما ويحاولون أن يلهبوا فيهم عاطفة الحب لله سبحانه والحنين إلى رضاه ورغبة شديدة لإصلاح النفس وتغير الحال.

These Sufis were initiating people on Oneness and sincerity in following the *Sunnah* of the Prophet ﷺ and to repent from their sins and to be away from every disobedience of Allah the Exalted. Their guides were encouraging them to move in the way of perfect Love to Allah the Exalted.

---

[110]*Risā'il Ibn 'Abidīn*, pp. 172 & 173.

[111]*Majallat al-Muslim*, 6th ed. 1378 A.H., p. 24.

[112]*Majallat al-Manār*, 1st year, p. 726.

...In Calcutta India, every day more than one thousand people were taking initiation into Sufism...by the influence of these Sufi people, thousands and thousands and hundreds of thousands in India found their Lord and reached a state of Perfection through the Islamic religion.[113]

MAULANA ABUL `ALA MAUDOODI (1321 - 1399 A.H.)

أما التصوف فيبحث عما كان في قلبه من الإخلاص وصفاء النية وصدق الطاعة عند قيامه بهذه الأعمال

Taṣawwuf searched for the sincerity in the heart and the purity in the intention and the trustworthiness in obedience in an individual's actions.[114]

[113] *Muslims in India*, pp. 140-146.
[114] *Mabadi' al-Islām*, p. 17.

Glossary

ʿabd (pl. *ʿibād*): lit. slave; servant.
ʿAbdAllāh: Lit., "servant of God"
Abū Bakr aṣ-Ṣiddīq: the closest Companion of Prophet Muḥammad; the Prophet's father-in-law, who shared the *Hijrah* with him. After the Prophet's death, he was elected the first caliph (successor); known as one of the most saintly Companions.
Abū Yazīd/Bayāzīd Bistāmī: A great ninth century *walī* and a master of the Naqshbandi Golden Chain.
adab: good manners, proper etiquette.
adhān: call to prayer.
Ākhirah: the Hereafter; Afterlife.
al-: Arabic definite article, "the".
ʿalāmīn: world; universes.
Alḥamdūlillāh: praise God.
ʿAlī ibn Abī Ṭālib: first cousin of Prophet Muḥammad, married to his daughter Fāṭimah; the fourth caliph.
alif: first letter of Arabic alphabet.
ʿAlīm, al-: the Knower, a divine attribute
Allāh: proper name for God in Arabic.
Allāhu Akbar: God is Greater.
ʿāmal: good deed (pl. *ʿamāl*).
amīr (pl., *umarā*): chief, leader, head of a nation or people.
anā: first person singular pronoun
anbīyā: prophets (sing. *nabī*).
ʿaql: intellect, reason; from the root *ʿaqila*: lit., "to fetter."
ʿArafah, ʿArafat: a plain near Mecca where pilgrims gather for the principal rite of Hajj.
ʿarif: knower, Gnostic; one who has reached spiritual knowledge of his Lord.
ʿĀrifūnʿ bil-Lāh: knowers of God.
Ar-Raḥīm: The Mercy-Giving, Merciful, Munificent, one of Allāh's ninety-nine Holy Names.
Ar-Raḥmān: The Most Merciful, Compassionate, Beneficent; the most repeated of Allāh's Holy Names.
ʿarsh, al-: the Divine Throne.
aṣl: root, origin, basis.
astāghfirullāh: lit. "I seek Allāh's forgiveness."
Awlīyāullāh: saints of Allāh (sing. *walī*).
āyah (pl. *ayāt*): a verse of the Holy Qur'an.
Āyat al-Kursī: "Verse of the Throne," a well-known supplication from the Qur'an (2:255).
ʿAzraʾīl: the Archangel of Death.
Badīʿ al-: The Innovator; a Divine Name.
Banī Ādam: Children of Adam; humanity.
Bayt al-Maqdis: the Sacred Mosque in Jerusalem, built at the site where Solomon's Temple was later erected.
Bayt al-Mā'mūr: much-frequented house; this refers to the Kaʿbah of the Heavens, which is the prototype of the Kaʿbah on Earth, circumambulated by the angels.
bayaʿ: pledge; in the context of this book, the pledge of initiation of a disciple (*murīd*) to a shaykh.
Bismillāhi'r-Raḥmāni'r-Raḥīm: "In the name of the All-Merciful, the All-Compassionate"; introductory verse to all chapters of the Qur'an, except the ninth.

Dajjāl: the False Messiah (Anti-Christ) will appear at the end-time of this world, to deceive Mankind with false divinity.
dalālah: evidence.
dhāt: self / selfhood.
dhawq (pl. *adhwāq*): tasting; technical term referring to the experiential aspect of gnosis.
dhikr: remembrance, mention of God in His Holy Names or phrases of glorification.
dīyā: light.
Diwān al-Awlīyā: the nightly gathering of saints with Prophet Muḥammad in the spiritual realm.
du'ā: supplication.
dunyā: world; worldly life.
'Eid: festival; the two major celebrations of Islam are 'Eid al-Fitr, after Ramaḍān; and 'Eid al-Adha, the Festival of Sacrifice during the time of Hajj, which commemorates the sacrifice of Prophet Abraham.
fard: obligatory worship.
Fātiḥah: Sūratu 'l-Fātiḥah; the opening chapter of the Qur'an.
Ghafūr, al-: The Forgiver; one of the Holy Names of God.
Ghawth: lit. "Helper"; the highest rank of all saints.
ghaybu' l-muṭlaq, al-: the Absolute Unknown; known only to God.
ghusl: full shower/bath obligated by a state of ritual impurity, performed before worship.
Grandshaykh: generally, a *walī* of great stature. In this text, refers to Mawlana 'AbdAllāh ad-Daghestāni (d. 1973), Mawlana Shaykh Nazim's master.
hā': the Arabic letter ه
ḥadīth Nabawī (pl., *aḥadīth*): prophetic tradition whose meaning and linguistic expression are those of Prophet Muḥammad.
Ḥadīth Qudsī: divine saying whose meaning directly reflects the meaning God intended but whose linguistic expression is not divine speech as in the Qur'an.
ḥadr: present
Hajj: the sacred pilgrimage of Islam obligatory on every mature Muslim once in their life.
ḥalāl: permitted, lawful according to Islamic *Sharī'ah.*
Ḥaqīqah, al-: reality of existence; ultimate truth.
ḥaqq: truth
Ḥaqq, al-: the Divine Reality, one of the 99 Divine Names.
ḥarām: forbidden, unlawful.
ḥasanāt: good deeds.
hāshā: God forbid.
ḥarf: (pl. *ḥurūf*) letter; Arabic root "edge."
Ḥawā: Eve.
ḥaywān: animal.
Hijrah: emigration.
ḥikmah: wisdom.
ḥujjah: proof.
hūwa: the pronoun "he,"made up of the Arabic letters *hā'* and *wāw.*
'ibādu 'l-Lāh: servants of God.
'ifrīt: a type of *jinn,* huge and powerful.
iḥsān: doing good, "It is to worship God as though you see Him; for if you are not seeing Him, He sees you."
ikhlāṣ, al-: sincere devotion.
ilāh: (pl. *āliha*): idols or gods.
ilāhīyya: divinity.

ilhām: divine inspiration sent to *awlīyāullāh.*
ʿilm: knowledge, science.
ʿIlmu ʾl-Awrāq: Knowledge of Papers.
ʿIlmu ʾl-Adhwāq: Knowledge of Taste.
ʿIlmu ʾl-Hurūf: Science of Letters.
ʿilmu ʾl-kalām: scholastic theology.
ʿilmun ladunnī: divinely inspired knowledge.
imān: faith, belief.
imām: leader of congregational prayer; an advanced scholar followed by a large community.
insān: humanity; pupil of the eye.
insānu ʾl-kāmil, al-: the Perfect Man, *i.e.*, Prophet Muḥammad.
irādatullāh: the Will of God.
irshād: spiritual guidance.
ism: name.
isma-Llāh: name of God.
isrāʿ: night journey; used here in reference to the night journey of Prophet Muḥammad.
Isrāʿfil: Archangel Rafael, in charge of blowing the Final Trumpet.
jalāl: majesty.
jamāl: beauty.
jamaʿa: group, congregation.
Jannah: Paradise.
jihād: to struggle in God's Path.
Jibrīl: Gabriel, Archangel of revelation.
Jinn: a species of living beings created from fire, invisible to most humans. *Jinns* can be Muslim or non-Muslim.
Jumuʿah: Friday congregational prayer, held in a large mosque.
Kaʿbah: the first House of God, located in Mecca, Saudi Arabia to which pilgrimage is made and to which Muslims face in prayer.
kāfir: unbeliever.
Kalāmullāh al-Qadīm: lit., Allāh's Ancient Words, *viz.* the Holy Qur'an.
kalīmat at-tawḥīd: lā ilāha illa-Llāh: "There is no god but Al-Lāh (the God)."
karāmat: miracles.
khalīfah: deputy.
Khāliq, al-: the Creator, one of 99 Divine Names.
khalq: Creation.
khāniqah: designated smaller place for worship other than a mosque; *zāwiyah.*
khuluq: conduct, manners.
Kirāmun Kātabīn: honored Scribe angels.
lā: no; not; not existent; the particle of negation.
lā ilāha illa-Llāh Muḥammadun Rasūlullāh: There is no deity except Allāh, Muḥammad is the Messenger of Allāh.
lām: Arabic letter ل.
al-Lawḥ al-Maḥfūẓ: the Preserved Tablets.
Laylat al-Isrāʿ wa'l-Miʿrāj: the Night Journey and Ascension of Prophet Muḥammad to Jerusalem and to the Seven Heavens.
Madīnātu ʾl-Munawwara: the Illuminated city; city of Prophet Muḥammad; Madinah.
mahr: dowry, given by the groom to the bride.
Malakūt: Divine Kingdom.
Malik, al-: the Sovereign, a Divine Name.
Mālik: Archangel of Hell.
maqām: spiritual station; tomb of a prophet, messenger or saint.
maʿrifah: gnosis.
Māshāʾ Allāh: as Allāh Wills.

Mawlānā: lit. "Our master" or "our patron,"referring to an esteemed person.
maƸhar: place of disclosure.
miḥrāb: prayer niche.
Mikāʿīl: Michael, Archangel of rain.
mīzān: the scale that weighs our deeds on Judgment Day.
mīm: Arabic letter م.
minbar: pulpit.
Miracles: of saints, known as *karamāt*; of prophets, known as *muʿjizāt* (lit., "That which renders powerless or helpless").
miʿrāj: the ascension of Prophet Muḥammad from Jerusalem to the Seven Heavens.
Muḥammadun rasūlu ʾl-Lāh: Muḥammad is the Messenger of God.
mulk, al-: the World of dominion.
Muʿmin, al-: Guardian of Faith, one of the 99 Names of God.
muʿmin: a believer.
munājāt: invocation to God in a very intimate form.
Munkir: one of the angels of the grave.
murīd: disciple, student, follower.
murshid: spiritual guide; *pir*.
mushāhadah: direct witnessing.
mushrik (pl. *mushrikūn*): idolater; polytheist.
muwwāḥid (pl. *muwāḥḥidun*): those who affirm God's Oneness.
nabī: a prophet of God.
nafs: lower self, ego.
Nakīr: the other angel of the grave (with Munkir).
nūr: light.
Nūḥ: the prophet Noah.
Nūr, an-: "The Source of Light"; a Divine Name.
Qādir, al-: "The Powerful"; a Divine Name.
qalam, al-: the Pen.
qiblah: direction, specifically, the direction faced by Muslims during prayer and other worship, towards the Sacred House in Mecca.
Quddūs, al-: "The Holy One"; a Divine Name.
qurb: nearness
quṭb (pl. *aqṭāb*): axis or pole. Among the poles are:
Quṭbu ʾl-Bilād: Pole of the Lands.
Quṭbu ʾl-Irshād: Pole of Guidance.
Quṭbu ʾl-Aqṭāb: Pole of Poles.
Quṭbu ʾl-Aʿz ham: Highest Pole.
Quṭbu ʾl-Mutaṣarrif: Pole of Affairs.
al-quṭbīyyatu ʾl-kubrā: the highest station of poleship.
Rabb, ar-: the Lord.
Raḥīm, ar-: "The Most Compassionate"; a Divine Name.
Raḥmān, ar-: "The All-Merciful"; a Divine Name.
raḥmā: mercy.
rakaʿat: one full set of prescribed motions in prayer. Each prayer consists of a one or more *rakaʿats.*
Ramaḍān: the ninth month of the Islamic calendar; month of fasting.
Rasūl: a messenger of God.
Rasūlullāh: the Messenger of God, Muḥammad ﷺ.
Raʿūf, ar-: "The Most Kind"; a Divine Name.
Razzāq, ar-: "The Provider"; a Divine Name.
rawḥānīyyah: spirituality; spiritual essence of something.
Riḍwān: Archangel of Paradise.
rizq: provision; sustenance.

rūḥ: spirit. *Ar-Rūḥ* is the name of a great angel.
rukū': bowing posture of the prayer.
ṣadaqah: voluntary charity.
Ṣaḥābah (sing., *ṣaḥābī*): Companions of the Prophet; the first Muslims.
ṣaḥīḥ: authentic; term certifying validity of a *ḥadīth* of the Prophet.
ṣāim: fasting person (pl. *ṣāimūn*)
sajda (pl. *sujūd*): prostration.
ṣalāt: ritual prayer, one of the five obligatory pillars of Islam. Also, to invoke blessing on the Prophet.
Ṣalāt an-Najāt: prayer of salvation, offered in the late hours of night.
ṣalawāt (sing. *ṣalāt*): invoking blessings and peace upon the Prophet.
salām: peace.
Salām, as-: "The Peaceful"; a Divine Name. *As-salāmu 'alaykum:* "Peace be upon you," the Islamic greeting.
Ṣamad, aṣ-: Self-Sufficient, upon whom creatures depend.
ṣawm, ṣiyām: fasting.
sayyi'āt: bad deeds; sins.
sayyid: leader; also, a descendant of Prophet Muḥammad.
Sayyīdinā: our master (fem. *sayyidunā; sayyidatunā*: our mistress).
shahādah: lit. testimony; the testimony of Islamic faith: *lā ilāha illa 'l-Lāh wa Muḥammadun rasūlu 'l-Lāh*, "There is no god but Allāh, the One God, and Muḥammad is the Messenger of God."
Shah Naqshband: Muḥammad Bahauddin Shah Naqshband, a great eighth century *walī*, and the founder of the Naqshbandi Ṭarīqah.
shaykh: lit. "old Man," a religious guide, teacher; master of spiritual discipline.
shifā': cure.
shirk: polytheism, idolatry, ascribing partners to God
ṣiffāt: attributes; term referring to Divine Attributes.
Silsilat adh-dhahabīyya: "Golden Chain"of spiritual authority in Islam
sohbet (Arabic, *suḥbah*): association: the assembly or discourse of a shaykh.
subḥānAllāh: glory be to God.
sulṭān/sulṭānah: ruler, monarch.
Sulṭān al-Awlīyā: lit., "King of the *awlīyā;* the highest-ranking saint.
Sūnnah: Practices of Prophet Muḥammad in actions and words; what he did, said, recommended, or approved of in his Companions.
sūrah: a chapter of the Qur'an; picture, image.
Sūratu 'l-Ikhlāṣ: Chapter 114 of Holy Qur'an; the Chapter of Sincerity.
ṭabīb: doctor.
tābi'īn: the Successors, one generation after the Prophet's Companions.
tafsīr: to explain, expound, explicate, or interpret; technical term for commentary or exegesis of the Holy Qur'an.
tajallī (pl. *tajallīyāt*): theophanies, God's self-disclosures, Divine Self-manifestation.
takbīr: lit. *"Allāhu Akbar,"*God is Great.
tarawīḥ: the special nightly prayers of Ramaḍān.
ṭarīqat/ṭarīqah: lit., way, road or path. An Islamic order or path of discipline

and devotion under a guide or shaykh; Sufism.

taṣbīḥ: recitation glorifying or praising God.

tawāḍaʿ: humbleness.

ṭawāf: the rite of circumambulating the Kaʿbah while glorifying God during Hajj and ʿUmra.

tawḥīd: unity; universal or primordial Islam, submission to God, as the sole Master of destiny and ultimate Reality.

Tawrāt: Torah

tayammum: Alternate ritual ablution performed in the absence of water.

ʿubūdīyyah: state of worshipfulness; servanthood.

ʿulamā (sing. *ʿālim*): scholars.

ʿulūmu ʿl-awwalīna wa ʿl-ākhirīn: Knowledge of the "Firsts"and the "Lasts" refers to the knowledge God poured into the heart of Prophet Muḥammad during his Holy Ascension to the Divine Presence.

ʿulūm al-Islāmī: Islamic religious sciences.

Ummāh: faith community, nation.

ʿUmar ibn al-Khaṭṭāb: an eminent Companion of Prophet Muḥammad and second caliph of Islam.

ʿumra: the minor pilgrimage to Mecca, performed at any time of the year.

ʿUthmān ibn ʿAffān: eminent Companion of the Prophet; his son-in-law and third caliph of Islam, renowned for compiling the Qur'an.

walad: a child.

waladī: my child.

walāyah: proximity or closeness; sainthood.

walī (pl. *awlīyā*): saint, or "he who assists"; guardian; protector.

wasīlah: a means; holy station of Prophet Muḥammad as God's intermediary to grant supplications.

wāw: Arabic letter و

wujūd, al-: existence; "to find," "the act of finding," and "being found."

Yʿaqūb: Jacob; the prophet.

yamīn: the right hand; previously meant "oath."

Yawm al-ʿahdi waʿl-mīthāq: Day of Oath and Covenant, a heavenly event before this Life, when all souls of humanity were present to God, and He took from each the promise to accept His Sovereignty as Lord.

yawm al-qiyāmah: Day of Judgment.

Yūsuf: Joseph; the prophet.

zāwiyah: designated smaller place for worship other than a mosque; also *khāniqah*.

zīyāra: visitation to the grave of a prophet, a prophet's companion or a saint.

Other Publications at isn1.net

Shaykh Muhammad Nazim Adil al-Haqqani

- We Have Honored the Children of Adam (2013)
- Heavenly Counsel: from Darkness into Light (2013)
- Heavenly Showers (2012)
- The Sufilive Series (6 vols.) (2010-12)
- Breaths from Beyond the Curtain
- Through the Eye of the Needle
- Eternity: Inspirations from Heavenly Sources
- The Path to Spiritual Excellence
- In the Mystic Footsteps of Saints (2) (also in ebook format)
- Liberating the Soul (6vols.)
- The Divine Kingdom

Shaykh Muhammad Hisham Kabbani

- The Benefits of Bismillah 'ir-Rahman 'ir-Raheem & Surat al-Fatihah (2013)
- The Importance of Prophet Muhammad in Our Daily Life (2013)
- The Hierarchy of Saints (2013)
- The Heavenly Power of Divine Obedience and Gratitude (2013)
- Salawat of Tremendous Blessings (2012, *Turkish/Spanish*)
- The Dome of Provisions (2012)
- The Prohibition of Domestic Violence in Islam (2011/*Fatwa*)
- The Sufilive Series (6) (2010-12)
- Jihad: Principles of Leadership in War and Peace (2010) (also in French)
- Cyprus Summer Series (2) (2009)
- The Nine-fold Ascent (2008)
- Who Are the Guides? (2008)
- Illuminations (2007)
- Banquet for the Soul (2006)
- Symphony of Remembrance
- The Healing Power of Sufi Meditation
- In the Shadow of Saints
- Keys to the Divine Kingdom
- The Sufi Science of Self-Realization (*also in French, Italian, Spanish*)
- Universe Rising
- The Approach of Armageddon (*also in French*)
- Pearls and Coral (2 vols)
- Classical Islam and the Naqshbandi Sufi Tradition
- The Naqshbandi Sufi Way
- Links of Light: The Golden Chain
- The Encyclopedia of Islamic Doctrine (7 volumes, 3 in French)
- Angels Unveiled, a Sufi Perspective (*also in Spanish*)
- Encyclopedia of Muḥammad's Women Companions and the Traditions They Related

Hajjah Amina Adil

- Muhammad: the Messenger of Islam (2001)
- The Light of Muhammad
- Lore of Light (3 vol.) / My Little Lore of Light
- Links of Light

Hajjah Naziha Adil Kabbani

- Heavenly Foods (2011)
- Secrets of Heavenly Food (2009)

www.ingramcontent.com/pod-product-compliance
Lightning Source LLC
Chambersburg PA
CBHW060501080526
44584CB00015B/1508
* 9 7 8 1 9 3 8 0 5 8 2 1 9 *